T0194648

Flights of Destiny

One going west and another east ...

...yet both involve the miracle power of

the God who cares

Lisa Bate

WESTBOW
PRESS®
A DIVISION OF THOMAS NELSON
& ZONDERVAN

WestBow Press books may be ordered through booksellers or by contacting:

WestBow Press
A Division of Thomas Nelson & Zondervan
1663 Liberty Drive
Bloomington, IN 47403
www.westbowpress.com
844-714-3454

ISBN: 978-1-9736-6580-9 (sc)
ISBN: 978-1-9736-6579-3 (hc)
ISBN: 978-1-9736-6581-6 (e)

Library of Congress Control Number: 2019907583

Print information available on the last page.

WestBow Press rev. date: 02/03/2021

FORWARD

It is an honor and a privilege to write this Forward.

I met Lisa in 1994 sitting on a bleacher, in a gym, watching Mary, Lisa's daughter, and my daughter, Holly, perform with the Hot Dog USA Jump Rope Team. From that moment on, I knew that Lisa would be someone special in my life and a real kindred spirit!

We traveled across the US and parts of Europe with the jump rope team, rooming together and becoming lifelong friends. It was on such an adventure that I first heard the story of Mary and Michael and realized that this life changing story needed to be told to and heard by as many people as possible. And when I told my husband, Tom, he agreed.

This is a modern day, Old Testament-type of miraculous story. A story full of unbelievable miracles that has encouraged me countless times, renewed my faith when I was faltering, and reminded me that God truly does specialize in things thought impossible.

So, thank you, Lisa, for sharing this story, your heart, and your friendship with me. I am blessed beyond measure and I'm a better person because of you!

Denise Diffee

Co-founder and Board member of Sycamore Tree Theater company, co-writer and co-producer of the musicals *Katie's Hope*, *A Light in the Attic* and *Unto the Hills*.

"*This book is filled with heart-wrenching trials, gripping adventures, and astounding miracles! Lisa Bate beautifully weaves the backstories of her family and several key people, to demonstrate how GOD can easily connect you with anyone -- even thousands of miles away, and HE is a miracle-working Father with Whom you can trust every single area of your life.*"

~Jackie Morey, International Bestselling Author | CEO of Customer Strategy Academy | Book Publisher | Business Strategist | Executive Coach.

CONTENTS

PART 5: CANCER

PART 6: STUNNING DEVELOPMENTS

INTRODUCTION

Twelve years ago I was told that my twenty-year-old son had stage-four cancer in the form of a huge tumor in his head. As with everyone, life throws us the unexpected, and sometimes it comes in frightening forms. In this book I will tell you a story of love and perseverance, and of God's supernatural involvement. It is a true story of how God journeys alongside us through the good times and the bad, including when we are hit with overwhelming problems much too big to solve ourselves.

Years ago I began keeping a journal, which included notes, calendars, and documents. My initial reason was that our children might someday treasure it and be reminded of how God worked in our lives. Memories fade with time and can be lost easily within just one generation. My intention was to organize our lives in writing to preserve our children's heritage for them, which also included Romanian adoptions, chance meetings, new friends in unusual places and powerful prayers. Later we decided to share our story with others as well.

The message I would most like to convey is that when facing seemingly impossible circumstances, rather than turning our backs on God out of frustration or fear, which is easy to fall into, or leaving Him out of the equation altogether, we would make the choice to turn to Him and include Him. He is never the enemy. He is our friend and helper in every situation. And when we turn to Him, we must not give up too soon, because circumstances can look much worse before they get better. I have chosen both ways at different times—without God and with God. I have learned which one is best. He cares. He is always on our side and can turn the impossible into possible. Jesus makes a way where there is no way.

"We will tell the next generation about the Lord's power and great deeds and the miraculous things he has done" (Psalm 78:4b God's Word Translation).

Dedicated to the memory of Jeffrey Sampson,
the man on the airplane.

I've lived in Communist Romania in the 70's and 80's. Nobody liked it but complied out of fear. When the regime took over in the 50's, they came and took everything from people who had things like land, horses, herds of animals, more than one house...in the name of equality and common wealth.

There were the secret police living in beautiful fenced houses, with all commodities and food delivery. They had separate, high-fenced resorts too. And then there were the common people standing in lines for food.

The communists also persecuted people who took their faith in God seriously. They came to the churches, took away the Bibles, interrogated the leaders and told them what they should believe. Mail was intercepted, phone calls were recorded and people disappeared. And I have described very little.

Daniela Potra

PART
ONE

Lenuta

Let God's promises shine on your problems.
—Corrie Ten Boom

CHAPTER 1

The Story Begins

THIS TRUE STORY BEGINS A half a world away in a mountain house above a small remote village in the communist country of Romania. It was there a baby girl was born to a poor farming family, far from privilege or the finer things that life hands out to other baby girls. Although much of the world was enjoying the modern times of the 1970s and '80s with its freedoms, inventions, technology, travel, and prosperity, this was not so in the small village of Somesu Rece, and even less so in this little isolated home high in the hills.

The people of Romania were oppressed under the control of the vicious dictator Nicolae Ceausescu. He had neither compassion nor conscience, it seemed, and he rivaled those who ruled throughout history with cruelty, greed, and hatred. He controlled the people by rationing food, electricity, and fuel; by paying low wages for long, hard hours; and by infiltrating the population with secret informants. The people had become disheartened because they no longer had any influence or control over their government. Life was hard physically, but the toll it took on their souls was the hardest to bear.

Into this world, Lenuta was born, the third child in her family. Her parents had searched for some peace and security, so settling in the mountains, further away from the daily control of the government, seemed logical. Nevertheless, just as it was in the homes below, fear, weariness, despair, and hunger had long ago moved in and became part of the family. No one can say for sure how old Lenuta was when she first noticed the presence of these unwanted intruders, but as a teenager, she became more and more troubled.

Lenuta was a beautiful and loving child; as she grew, so did the family, as four more children were added to the already crowded home. She was also a bright and capable girl and so was depended upon for help with the cooking, the chores, and the younger children. It was necessary. This was not a time or a place for indulging childhood. This was an era when children grew up before their time. Many children who could not be fed and cared for could not stay with their families. They were taken to state-run orphanages. The government was rationing food and pay while, at the same time, making birth control illegal in order to create a larger future work force. *How can that possibly work?* wondered Lenuta. She became more aware of what was happening—and so did everyone else—but her thoughts and theirs remained mostly unspoken. Those who expressed such concerns—implying the government was misguided—could be beaten or imprisoned. She had heard of families who had taken their children to these facilities. They would go back and get their children, they said, when times were better, but times seldom were and the parents seldom did. Many times, they even had more children.

When the opportunity arose to move from the overcrowded house in the hills, Lenuta at age seventeen accepted the marriage proposal of a twenty-six-year-old man from the village below. She was not fleeing far, but it felt like an escape nonetheless. Gaby, Lenuta's new husband, proved to be resourceful. He did what few others had been able to do in the rural villages—he managed to acquire an automobile. It was cheaply made and had to be started with a crank in the front, but it was a distraction more than anything from day-to-day life, and Gaby enjoyed puttering with it.

Lenuta became pregnant right away, and in nine months' time, their daughter was born. About nine months after the birth of their baby girl, Lenuta discovered that she was expecting their second child.

It was during this time, on a cold icy day in December, when Lenuta was over eight months into her pregnancy and Gaby was out working on the car, that the unthinkable was about to take place and change destinies in a moment. Gaby, wishing to start up his car, engaged in a practice he had learned from other villagers. He took his pan of diesel fuel into their home to heat on the wood stove just inside the door. As the diesel heated, the house filled with fumes. It all happened quickly. Lenuta protested the fumes, so Gaby picked up the pan of heated fuel and as he was stepping outside he slipped on the ice and tumbled to the ground, dousing himself with diesel. Because of the close proximity of the wood stove, the fuel ignited, setting both Gaby and his home on fire. Neighbors came running, some to the front to help Gaby and some to the back to try to help Lenuta and her little daughter escape the burning home. With fire engulfing the front of the home, where the only exit was, Lenuta broke the glass in the tiny window in the back of the house and handed her child to neighbors. It was an incredible feat that they were able to get Lenuta out that window at all, but they did, which caused her labor to begin. And, so, her second child, a son, came into the world.

Lenuta was now homeless as her house had burned to the ground on that frozen December day. She and her children moved into the small home of one of Gaby's sisters and her family. For the next three months, Gaby agonizingly lingered between life and death in a dreary hospital room with Lenuta continuously by his side. Leaving their eighteen-month-old daughter and newborn son in the care of Gaby's frightened and heartbroken relatives tugged at her heart, and she feared for the effects that the magnitude of this grief would bring upon her children. She was also keenly aware that the sudden absence of their parents, especially in their daughter's life, could be taking some sort of negative emotional toll.

Finally, the badly burned Gaby could fight no longer. He slipped away, leaving Lenuta to fend for herself and her children. After some time had passed, Lenuta felt her sister-in-law's home was so crowded that she considered the opportunity to move in with a man in the village named Gheorghe, who was more than twenty years her senior.

It was a decision driven by desperation for the survival of the young family, and Gheorghe did possess a home with a barn, a well, a horse, a cow, chickens, and plenty of room for a large garden. These things were invaluable commodities in Romania since houses and land were primarily acquired through family inheritance, most commonly passed down to the boys.

CHAPTER 2

Starting Again

HAVING FELT A GROWING AND deep sense of anxiety and dread, but now with a plan in mind, Lenuta and her children could start a new life. And so they did, but once again for Lenuta, real life did not mirror her dreams or her imagination. All too soon she found Gheorghe to be difficult and then abusive, and even more so after they married. He constantly drank, was barraged with health problems, and was angered by the presence of Lenuta's children. Soon she discovered she was pregnant, and she hoped this new life would bring him some peace and happiness with which to appease whatever was creating such hostility.

After a year, the situation was becoming unbearable, and when she became pregnant with her fourth child, Gheorghe's abuse toward her two oldest children elevated to much larger threats. She began to fear for their lives and was in terror that he would make good on his threats and that, once she entered the hospital to have her baby, he would sell them perhaps to passing nomads or on the black market and she would never know what fate had befallen them.

Lenuta had never felt so alone. She began to search her surroundings and her heart for meaning. The beauty, purpose, and safety that should accompany life had persistently eluded hers, but certainly must exist somewhere, she thought. There was the obvious beauty in the blue gem-colored sky and in the bubbly racing river at the foot of the hill, and a certain tranquility in the livestock that grazed the hillside, and so she turned her focus toward God, who had created such beauty with the hope He could bring some into her life. He was, after all, Emmanuel, God with us (Mathew 1:23), even here and now in her desperate situation. And, so, with a new peace and confidence that went deep into her soul, Lenuta spent many hours calling out to God to save her children.

At about this time, a revolution was beginning to brew in Romania as oppression had escalated to an excruciating level, ending December 25, 1989, with the overthrow, trial, and execution of Nicolae Ceausescu and his wife. The hunger of the people for joining life outside their country caused the borders to open and the media swarmed in. The conditions of life in Romania for its citizens, as well as the multitude of abandoned children discovered housed in state-run orphanages, caused an outrage that was televised around the world. The Romanian government opened these orphanages for international adoptions, though the laws to do so were strict.

PART
TWO

Plight of the Orphans

The Starfish Story
Original Story by Loren Eisley

One day a man noticed a boy gently throwing something
into the ocean. "What are you doing?" he asked.

"Throwing starfish back into the ocean before they die."

"Don't you realize there are miles of beach and hundreds
of starfish? You can't make a difference," the man said.

Listening politely, the boy picked up another starfish and threw
it back into the surf. "It made a difference for that one," he said.

CHAPTER 3

News from Romania

IT WAS **1990,** AND OUR fourteen-year-old son, Jon, was getting ready for his baseball tournament in Sequim. It was a two-hour drive from our home in Kirkland, a suburb of Seattle, to the little town on the peninsula. "We have less rainfall here in Sequim than they have in San Francisco," its community boasted. For a town in the Pacific Northwest, this was definitely a selling point for visiting.

"Jon, will you start taking some of these things to the car?" I asked. He would be pitching that day and was planning some strategy, and I could tell I was interrupting his thoughts. There wasn't too much— just a cooler, some blankets, folding chairs, and the movie camera. Although Jon was new this year to the team, Brian, Jon's dad, and I had met most of the parents throughout the season and were anticipating a lovely day. As it turned out, it was indeed. The games were fun to watch, and I found the conversation among the mothers of particular interest. Lately, the newspapers and television news shows had been filled with stories of the fall of an Eastern European communist dictator. As the horrors unfolded of life within Romania, the rest of the world reacted with shock and anger toward a government that could give so little yet demand so much of its citizens.

The news media was working hard to expose the tragic reign of the

Romanian ex-president, Nicolae Ceausescu. Numbered among these atrocities included the destruction to the land by pollution and the bulldozing and demolishing of old architectural buildings, which were likened to works of art and had been constructed during Romania's free and prosperous years before communism took hold. Also appalling was the severe rationing of food and other necessary products for comfortable and safe living. As these news stories were being discussed by the mothers during lulls in the games, the conversation turned toward a recently broadcast program that exposed the outrageous conditions behind those closed borders suffered by their tiniest and most vulnerable citizens. Some families were unable to feed or care for their children. The government promised to come to the aid of the families; however, their solution was to warehouse the children in government-operated orphanages. Although many of these children were not true orphans, having one or both parents still living, they were nevertheless turned over to the state to be fed and cared for. Other children were abandoned in the hospitals where they were born or left there later, many times unidentified. Most people did not send their children away, but many did out of necessity. Food was scarce and perhaps they didn't realize what the conditions were like inside the orphanages.

As the media continued to focus and probe into the conditions of life within the orphanages, hearts broke around the world as the footage appeared on their television screens. The power of these pictures brought into reality the stories that had been written in the newspapers. Right before the eyes of the world were abandoned and lonely children living in squalor, prisoners in their own cribs. These children had long ago learned not to cry for there was no one to pick them up, talk to them, or play with them. Some of the children were tied to their cribs, restrained with sheets, and their diapers were rarely changed. Many of them were malnourished, dehydrated, sick with diarrhea and other illnesses, and slept with blankets infested with lice. We found out later that many of these children had contracted AIDS from transfusions given to them in the orphanages with the misconception that the tainted blood was full of nutrients.

We all agreed that, of all the frightful events and conditions that had been forced upon that country, the plight of the orphans seemed most dreadful of all. As the days went on, the reports kept coming, and the public became riveted by the information that continued to surface. Now that the regime had fallen, European and American advisors were allowed to travel into the country to help foreign aid organizations facilitate adoptions. The subsequent top news stories were about Americans and Europeans who were travelling to Romania desiring to adopt some of these institutionalized children.

CHAPTER 4

Thoughts of Adoption

As BRIAN AND I PONDERED these events and heard individual stories of people who had gone to Romania and adopted, we began wondering about the possibility of doing the same. After all, we had one fourteen-year-old son, and there could be room for another child. How would life change for Jon, having been the only child his entire life? Adopting a child would have a major impact on him. From the first day of discussing it, however, Jon was very interested and in favor of learning more. We decided to look into the possibilities and find out what steps were involved and where we should begin if we should decide to do so. The three of us were very close, so we were definitely not taking the choice to add another family member lightly. We would ask God and trust that He would open or shut the door at any step. With all this in mind, we felt confident in moving ahead.

Brian needed a van for his business. He looked in the classified section of the newspaper and found one that would work just fine. He called the owner and made an appointment for the following day to meet and check out the van. When Brian arrived, the owner of the van introduced himself as Cornell Petrisor. He was a young man with an accent that Brian was unfamiliar with, so he asked Cornell what country he was from. To his surprise, the reply was Romania. Cornell continued on to tell Brian an amazing story of how he had escaped communist Romania six years earlier when he was just twenty-one. Brian, in turn, told Cornell about the possibility that we might adopt a child from Romania. Brian bought the van from Cornell, but not without Cornell setting up a time for us to join him and his wife, Rodica, at their home for dinner.

The evening at Cornell and Rodica's home turned out to be very informative as well as a lot of fun. They were an enjoyable couple, and even though Rodica had not been in the United States for long and had not yet learned English, we picked up on her sweet spirit immediately. It was a fascinating evening. Cornell told us stories of growing up in Romania and why he had been willing to risk his life escaping his homeland to an unknown future with the very real possibility of never again seeing his family and friends or the little village he grew up in.

Cornell told us that his father was a pastor at the Pentecostal church in a rural village and was a respected man to whom people had turned for help and encouragement during the brutal years of communism. His mother was a kind, hardworking, and nurturing woman, but even with good parents, life was a strain. Cornell remembered one of his jobs as a young child, around the age of seven. He had to bring the cows home from their grazing spot on the hill. He would have to walk through the pitch-dark forest herding the cows by himself and was terrified every evening of the sounds and the shadows. His childhood was filled with adult responsibilities, and because of his discontentment, he left home at age fourteen. He moved to the nearby city of Cluj-Napoca where he got a job as a waiter.

Every young man in Romania was required to enlist in the army, and the time came for Cornell to join. Being an energetic and hard worker, he quickly rose to a position of head waiter, serving meals to the officers of the army. He also held the key to the reserves, mainly the food, so he had a lot of responsibility, and risk came with it. The president, Ceausescu, would also come in to be served at times, and being a sociopath, who could promote one day and murder the same individual the following day, he was not someone anyone wished to serve. His family members would come in also. They, too, were merciless, corrupt, and unpredictable. Cornell, working in such close proximity to this family, knew the dangers his position held, and he made the decision to escape the country once and for all. He had considered it many times before, but now it was crucial.

He let his parents know and then took off into the night. The first part of his escape route took him southeast toward the Danube River. He hiked through the dense woods and swam the river. In order to avoid being shot by the Romanian border guards, he swam underwater, concealed by some floating vegetation while breathing through a small tube. After making it across the Danube, he ended up in what was then Yugoslavia, but if caught there, he would have been sent back to Romania to face imprisonment or worse. He once again had to hike through miles of woods. This time he was cold, his feet were blistered, and he was wet and hungry. He was able to finally make it to Italy where he went to the United States Embassy and pleaded for political asylum.

Cornell finally was able to get his visa to the United States and decided first to settle in the Chicago area. He later made the move to Seattle where there were lots of employment opportunities and a large Romanian community. He worked hard as a tile setter and saved what he could. The years passed quickly until one day, in December 1989, he heard on the news of a revolution taking place in Romania. He listened carefully to glean all the details and was encouraged at what he heard. On December 16, Romanian government security forces attacked and killed civilian protestors in the Transylvanian town of Timisoara and then killed hundreds more the following day. This triggered a revolution and protests began in Bucharest. The police were instructed to shoot into these crowds. By December 22, President Ceausescu fled Bucharest as the fighting broke out between his security forces and the civilians, with whom the army had sided. Ceausescu and his forces were no match for an angry population with an army stepping in to aid them. Events were unfolding at a rapid pace, and the hunt for Ceausescu had now become top priority. The army was quickly able to defeat Ceausescu's internal security forces and Ceausescu and his wife, Elena, who had ruled alongside him, were captured on

December 23. They were tried and convicted of genocide and abuses of power and were both executed on December 25. A temporary interim government was put in place with Ion Iliescu in charge.

Cornell wanted to visit Romania, and we made an agreement with him. He would go with us and be our translator. When details were agreed upon, we all began fine tuning our plans for the trip. Cornell recommended bringing Jon along, assuring Brian and me that the areas we would be travelling in would be safe. We grilled Cornell on this, wanting to make absolutely sure this would be the case. We preferred that Jon come with us; however, it had not been long since Romania had been a very dangerous place to be for anyone. The country suffered from poverty, crime, black market activity, and lingering communistic mindsets in the police force and government. Cornell and Rodica assured us we would be traveling in areas Cornell was familiar with, that he knew many people in those places, and that he knew it to be safe. He said we would all be staying with his family and there was no need for apprehension. Once we were convinced this was a safe decision, we were excited to be taking Jon. An adoption would obviously impact his world dramatically, and we were both happy to think that Jon would be able to give his input.

It was a bit scary thinking of going to Transylvania, a northern area of Romania. In 1897, Irishman Bram Stoker wrote a book, *Dracula*, set in Transylvania. His book was fiction; however, it was based on an actual ruler named Dracula who lived in the fifteenth century. There have been many different versions and remakes of movies based on Stoker's horror novel, which took place in "the country beyond the forest." Getting to know Cornell and Rodica, former residents of Transylvania, was working to rebrand the image in my mind from vampires, evil counts, crumbling castles, and deep dark forests, to families, farmlands, and day-to-day living.

Around this time the news reports pertaining to the adoptions grew more ominous as the Romanian government was preparing to shut them down to restructure the process—if they were to be continued on at all. The invasive reporting on the horrendous conditions of the orphanages had become a worldwide spectacle and an embarrassment to the Romanian government. The black-market agents trafficking children were becoming a terrible problem as well. The government's response was to begin the shutdown and set a final court date to allow enough time to wrap up the processes that had already begun. When we heard this, we knew the date of our departure must be moved up. We only hoped that the paperwork would be finalized and get to us in time. There was only one document we were waiting for from Immigration and Naturalization Service (INS), which was supposed to take up to three months to receive back. Our flight date was past the three-month time frame, so everything looked fine. I called INS and was assured again that we were approved, and the final paperwork should be in our hands by our scheduled departure, but when our flight was only two days out, I knew action needed to be taken.

CHAPTER 5

Worrisome Delay

I HAD BEEN AWARE FROM our social worker of the reputation of the particular INS director whom I needed to speak with, and I knew she could be difficult. Having a job such as this required her to deal with laws, protocol, and complicated issues of people desiring to immigrate and would require a certain amount of firmness. These very qualities, I'm sure, had gotten her into the prestigious position she held; however, she had a reputation for not only firmness but of tough, unbending authority.

During one of my many calls to INS, when I inquired about the whereabouts of our paperwork, I was instructed not to be concerned about having the document with us. The agent said to simply explain to those helping us at the US Embassy in Romania that we had not yet received the approved documents in the mail, so we did not have them with us. Oh, how I laughed to myself over that one. I silently played out in my mind her suggested scenario. A person had only to read the newspapers to know this was not an option. My resolve settled in as I reflected on how unsuccessful that conversation would be. I knew a personal visit to our director was necessary. The problem was that I doubted whether I would be permitted to see her. I felt certain no agent could help me, so I knew I needed to see the director. I had been to the INS building in Seattle multiple times during the lengthy process of getting approved for an international adoption. Without the approved documents in hand we would not be allowed to bring a child into the US.

Upon entering the INS building, I bypassed the familiar number machine and all the people waiting their turn. I was about to approach an employee about locating the director, when I saw her walking on the other side of the large room. She walked over to an unmarked door and entered the room, closing the door behind her. I bypassed the counter and knocked on the door. I heard her voice inviting me in. I opened the door, walked across the room, and sat down opposite her at her desk. Once we were face to face, I spilled out our dilemma to her disapproving expression. She scolded that we had no right to book a flight until we had received all of the necessary paperwork. Although her tone and words were reprimanding, she went to the files, pulled out some paperwork, and then did some signing, stamping, and recording. In only a few moments, I was proceeding toward the door with the documentation I had come for and wishes of good luck from the actually very helpful director.

Our little group began our long journey to Romania, starting in Seattle, stopping in Chicago, New York, Vienna, and finally arriving in Bucharest, Romania. It was in the New York airport that I had a moment of reflection on how much effort it had taken to get all we needed prepared and ready for the undertaking ahead, and it was also then that a solemn thought struck. I had been so preoccupied with the details for this trip that I had neglected my times alone with God. How was I to be sensitive to His leading when maybe I had been leaving Him out? It was critical we find His plan when we were in Romania and not concoct our own. It was then I heard Him as I felt He spoke to my heart that this was not about what I had or had not done; this was about what He was going to do. This was spoken so kindly, and it did not feel as though it was meant to reprove; rather it was said to remove the load from our shoulders and allow it to go into His powerful and loving hands. I felt happy and relieved thinking of the help He had promised, and hoped we would keep our trust in Him as we commenced in these tasks before us.

Stepping off of the plane in Romania was, to me, like stepping into a setting I might experience through the pages of a book or a movie. There were soldiers carrying large automatic rifles, and the close proximity of such large loaded guns was a new and unwelcome experience. It became even more surreal as the air was filled with Dracula-style harpsicord music. Even in those early days after the revolution, the Romanians knew the world was fascinated with Dracula and hoped to entice tourists to come and explore the mist-filled and mysterious Carpathian Mountain area of Transylvania where Dracula once roamed.

Added to the uncomfortable entrance, the airport was in disrepair. The windows and floors were dirty, and there were no plants or paintings or anything pleasant to the eye. There were no shop or restaurant owners trying to grab the attention of those passing by with bright signs and enticing products. This was actually not a tourist or citizen-friendly atmosphere in spite of the harpsicord music effort. Cornell seemed very comfortable with the surroundings because he was home. Jon was enjoying the adventure, and Cornell navigated us through the airport like a professional by offering cash to speed the process of getting the luggage through in a timely manner. The cash prevented a lengthy, unnecessary search, which often would result in the airport employees stealing items from the suitcases.

PART
THREE

Romania

I want to know God's thoughts. The rest are just details.
—Albert Einstein

CHAPTER 6

New Friends in Foreign Places

CORNELL'S BROTHER, DAVID, AND BROTHER-IN-LAW, Trion, picked us up from the airport in a van Cornell had previously purchased. So began a journey that was almost as long as the flight to Romania. The road trip was fascinating. We listened to the lively conversation in the Romanian language while we scanned the countryside. It felt as though we had landed in an era gone by, and indeed we had in some regards, as progress here had stopped years ago. There were horses and carts loaded with sticks and hay, ladies wearing scarves (*babushkas*) tied under their chins selling their needlework, and others selling their homegrown vegetables along the roadside. We passed villages in which each home was nestled in a little compound surrounded by walls and a gate. Inside the gate was a courtyard, barn, outhouse, and well all clustered close together.

We stopped at a restaurant, and while Cornell, Jon, Brian, and I laughed and talked, I couldn't help but notice the weariness and sadness on the faces of the people around me. It didn't take long to pick up on the trauma that was in the air. It seemed the joy and laughter had been stolen from these citizens by the ruthless leadership that had plundered them for so long. After about a twelve-hour drive, we arrived at the little village of Somesu Rece, which means "cold river" due to the fact it is situated on a beautiful river that was, of course, cold. This was a picturesque setting, and the surrounding hills were dotted with sheep grazing on the lush, grassy slopes. Cornell's family members were warm and inviting and provided us a room to sleep in. There was no plumbing or central heating, but it was cozy just the same, with the toasty wood stove performing perfectly as we drifted off to sleep after that very long day.

As dawn was barely beginning to break on our first morning in Somesu Rece, we could hear the clip clop of horses' hooves and the crunching of the wheels of the carts on the dirt roads outside our window. Even though it was still quite dark, many residents were already up taking their carts into the forest area to gather sticks and branches for firewood. Jobs were difficult, and Rodica's sister told us that the factory where she worked would, most always, have a reason why they could not pay the workers their full salaries, which were already meager. It was either that the employees had not achieved what was expected or the company had not sold enough product.

We were still quite exhausted from our long trip, so we dozed off to sleep once again. We awoke later to a delicious breakfast made by Cornell's mom and lots of smiles and welcome from his family and the visitors we met. All meals were started with the traditional blessing of *pofta buna*, which means "good appetite" similar to the French term, *bon appetite*. It is a blessing, so to speak, and a moment to acknowledge the good food as well as the company of those gathered around the table. Typically, the father would pronounce this blessing and then the diners would cheerfully echo his blessing, and so the meal began. I had practiced saying *multumesc* which is "thank you" in the Romanian language, and after my plate was empty and we were to be on our way, I attempted to communicate my thanks. Apparently, what I actually contributed was entertainment, as their laughter filled the air, and I was asked to repeat myself once again. Soon after the meal Cornell, Brian, Jon, and I piled into the van. We knew we must get our project underway as soon as possible because of the deadline for the adoptions.

First on the agenda was making the half-hour trip to Cluj-Napoca to contact a lawyer. Cluj-Napoca is the second largest city in Romania after Bucharest, and there we would find an attorney, translators, and all that we needed to make this process legal and expedited as quickly as possible. Cluj was a beautiful city, but the exquisite architectural designs and the immense skill and craftsmanship that it took to construct such buildings had not been valued for years. The leaders had not cared that these buildings were being destroyed little by little because of neglect, and what was even more shocking, they had actually bulldozed and replaced many of them with shoddily constructed high-rise apartments. These truly beautiful and historic old buildings were many years ago treasured masterpieces. To walk into them and see their high ceilings and delicately carved detailed woodwork on handrails and moldings was breathtaking. In one of these buildings I was mesmerized by the crown molding around the entire circumference of the room because it was intricately carved with violins and flowers. There was similar carving and artistry on the sweeping banisters, but sadly all was in disrepair. There were many light fixtures with burned-out light bulbs or even none at all. I went into the ladies' room in one of these extraordinary buildings only to find the toilet actually tipped over onto the floor. There was a sink but no running water and never any paper products. The ladies' room was completely useless, so I had to go into the men's when no one was there while Brian posted guard duty at the door. These buildings seemed to be telling their story—the Romanians were industrious and creative visionaries who once were prosperous. They were also telling the story of a communist government that had completely failed the people.

Cornell led the way down a long hallway, and soon we were walking into the lawyer's office, a room crowded with several desks. I was amazed at what I saw next as we walked past these work areas. This was 1991, yet here were manual typewriters that looked like they were from the 1950s or even earlier. We found nothing modern in this big government building. These well-dressed government professionals stationed at their desks with typewriters in front of them were typing using only their index fingers. They all typed in this manner and were surprisingly proficient at it. Although they did their best at dressing the part for their important jobs, the signs were there that clothing and accessories were not easy to acquire even for these employees. Men had fancy suits yet looked as if they had not been laundered for some time, and repairs were done with various unmatched colors of thread. In one instance, I noticed that a bright, almost fluorescent purple thread and magenta-colored zipper had been used to replace the original zipper on a man's gray suit.

As we continued to walk through the room, we came face to face with a handsome dark-haired man in his thirties behind a large wooden desk. Cornell quickly engaged in a long and spirited talk with this man, who apparently was going to be our attorney. Of course, the conversation was all in Romanian, but I was listening intently trying to hear something that would give me a clue as to the direction this was all going. Knowing no Romanian beside "pofta buna" and "multumesc," I was at a loss until I heard a word I was sure I could translate. It was *imposibil*. I was beginning to see where this was all going, but for some reason, it struck me as funny. Not because it truly didn't, at times, seem crazy and impossible, but because in my life and in the lives of others I knew, when things were impossible, God often, in so many instances, had stepped in and done something truly spectacular.

According to our new lawyer, the paperwork to be done was too much and the wait times too long. Even if we had already located a child, the last court date was too near. First of all, most of the abandoned children had living parents who needed to be tracked down so they could sign release forms. This would be daunting since the record keeping was quite hit and miss. There were also mounds of paperwork, meetings with various government officials and translators for the documents, waiting periods, interviews to take place, and more paperwork to be filled out, verified, and notarized.

Upon leaving the lawyer, we set out to one of the nearby orphanages to apparently attempt the "imposibil." As we approached the large facility, we were surprised at what we saw next. Posted outside the orphanage that housed so many abandoned and severely neglected children were soldiers in full uniform with automatic rifles. Until visiting Romania, I had never been so near soldiers armed with high-powered weapons that could be directed at me or my family at any moment. I had seen them first in the airport, and now there were more here at the orphanage. I reflected on the fact that the civilian population of Romania had lived under this frightening oppression for years. We began to see our lawyer's point about the "imposibil."

Cornell began speaking with the soldiers guarding this orphanage, and I was certain by their manner that we would not be allowed any further toward this building or these children. It was haunting to know what was taking place behind those walls and to be so close and yet so powerless to make a difference. These institutionalized children, unless some major change came about, were destined to live out their lives with no family or education. After reaching maturity, they would be sent to similar facilities for adults where they would be taught menial tasks for which they would be given little pay. For the most part, they would never be capable of mainstreaming into society at all. Our next destination was a local hospital where babies were often relinquished at birth or brought back later. It was unusual to find no abandoned children at any hospital, and we checked a few other places, but we found no good leads.

CHAPTER 7

Two Kids in the Village

DURING THIS TIME, CORNELL MENTIONED to us that two children from his village were in a desperate situation. They were ages three and four and were brother and sister. Their father had been killed in a tragic accident, and when the mother heard of us, she felt that surely we must be the answer to her prayers. This last part we didn't know, only that we would not take children from their mother or any other family member, especially older ones such as these. We agreed that this was not a possibility.

After following some other leads that didn't amount to anything, Cornell again mentioned the two children from his village who needed to move out of their home situation, and once again we felt this was not the avenue for us to take. After all, they were not languishing away alone and forgotten or neglected in an orphanage, but in a home with a mother, neighbors, and the freedom to play in the streets of their village. Certainly their lives would be far from perfect in a place such as this, but no one's life is perfect, and who is to say what makes a good life or what was ahead for this country that could be stepping into a new and brighter future.

We explored several new opportunities, but they all ended abruptly. Now for a third time the subject was brought up about the siblings in the village. This time a new thought process began in our minds. First of all, at the beginning of this adventure, we had prayed and were trusting that God would open and close doors to get us to where He wanted us to be. Certainly we had seen doors slam closed that had been wide open to others a very short time ago. Now there was a potentially open door, and it seemed that we were determined to avoid it altogether. We began contemplating the idea of exploring the possibilities of this lone option. We agreed to look into why the family members had persisted in wanting strangers to take the children knowing they would end up so far away. The kids would have to deal not only with a new family, but a different country and language as well.

After discussions back and forth, we all reached an agreement that an initial meeting should take place. Cornell explained to us the severity of the situation within the family. The stepfather was abusive and was threatening to get rid of the children—a three-year-old boy and a four-year-old girl. Others in the village expressed that he was deranged, that he would lock the kids in a dark cellar or banish them to the barn overnight. One night when the kids were banished to sleep in the barn loft, the stepfather climbed the ladder to get up to the kids. Who knows what his intentions were, but when he got to the top of the ladder, the little boy tried to kick him in the face, causing him to lose his balance, knocking the drunk, overweight man off the ladder. The next day the stepfather picked up the boy by the shirt, looked him in the eye, and told him that, if he ever did it again, he would kill him. The children's mother was desperate.

This put things in a much different perspective, but we also wondered why she was so frightened of her children disappearing without a trace, and yet here we were to make that happen. Why would she trust us? Cornell began answering our questions one by one. It was reassuring that we were travelling with him, who had grown up in the village. Additionally, Cornell apparently highly vouched for us, and he assured them that he lived near us in the United States and would be in contact with the children, so they would not, in fact, be lost to her forever.

We were all set to meet late in the afternoon at the home of Cornell's sister, Victoria. She invited us to come earlier and then served us a nice lunch with the help of her teenage daughter, Claudia. It was a wonderful time, and we also met Victoria's teenage son, Florin. Cornell was busy translating back and forth as we got to know them all a bit. The people of Somesu Rece were very hospitable, and we always felt welcome and comfortable when visiting their homes. It was certainly true on that day. Finally, the time had come, and Victoria answered a knock at the door. A young woman with two small children stepped through the doorway, and we were introduced to Lenuta and her children, Mariora and Gaby.

Lenuta's attire was similar to that of the other ladies in the village—a dress, an apron around her waist, leggings, and a scarf tied under her chin. We quickly discovered that, although we could not communicate directly with her through language, there was a warmth, pleasantness, and even a peace about her in this situation. The children were dressed in warm clothing with knit hats and received much attention from Claudia and Florin as they played, laughed, and talked with them. Meanwhile, Cornell began a conversation between us and their mother. He began by seeking to clarify the wishes of Lenuta and her reasoning behind those wishes. She was very open and laid her story out exactly as it had already been relayed to us. It was at this point the sorrow, anguish, and desperation she was carrying began to betray themselves upon her face as Cornell translated her words. She looked straight into our faces and eyes and asked if we would take her children to America.

We took in this moment, this story, this young mother, and these children. It wasn't a long discussion between Brian, Jon, and me that brought us to our decision. It seemed this path had been attempting to present itself from the moment we arrived on Romanian soil, and in fact even before. After all, what were the chances we would meet Cornell as we answered the newspaper ad for a van, or that he would offer to help and even come with us when we already had our plans in place. Yet here we were in this particular Romanian village with such a need before us and paperwork stamped with the approval from the INS in our possession.

The next moment will be etched in my mind forever. I could not look at Lenuta's face as Cornell gave her our answer, and I tried to imagine what she might be feeling. After all, it was one thing to pray for this rescue, but quite another to be faced with its reality and the people that would take the children away, very possibly forever. Now Brian and I had become that vehicle, and I feared to look at her face as her nightmare at home had brought her down this road.

I dared to take a glance, and what I witnessed was entirely unexpected, for there radiating from Lenuta's face at that defining, life-altering point in time was an expression of pure relief, gratitude, and even joy. The fear of her husband, Gheorghe, along with his threats, had weighed her down, and now he would lose his frightening grip once and for all. I felt tears stinging in my eyes and sadness to see the immensity of anguish that must have been accompanying her for such a long time. Cornell began right away speaking to the children about coming to America, which they seemed willing and delighted to do as there was always much buzz in the village about life in America. Of course, they were only three and four years old and had no comprehension about what any of this really meant and the drastic changes that would soon be taking place for them. Lenuta had already discussed with the kids these possibilities, and so they seemed to be prepared for the conversation that afternoon.

The Somesu Rece villagers seemed thrilled with the decision as news traveled quickly, for they had long been familiar with the situation and had sadly witnessed Lenuta's fear, heartbreak, and struggle. They also knew of her faith and many prayers on behalf of the children. It was funny, in a way, how God had gotten us to this village. And here we had been looking in every direction but this one. As if to put one more stamp of approval on this direction, Cornell asked the kids what they would like from these new parents. Gaby was having too much fun playing to pay any attention, but Mariora answered without hesitation that she wanted an *ursulet* and *ciocolată*. The translation? A teddy bear and chocolate. The one and only toy we had packed in our already overstuffed suitcases, besides a little homemade rag doll, was a wind-up musical teddy bear. We had also packed lots of chocolate and various other candies to give away. Brian hurried the couple of blocks back to our room and soon returned with the teddy bear and chocolate in hand. There was a wide-eyed look of amazement on Mariora's face as she was no doubt softening toward these new parents, who at this moment, must have seemed pretty spectacular granting her wish so quickly.

Cornell's parents and other family members had stopped by Cornell's other sister's home that evening where we were having dinner, and so the little home was full of kids and adults. Mariora and Gaby were brought over as well. It was a happy atmosphere with celebration in the air because of these recent events and agreements. There were still many hurdles ahead and deadlines to reach before the last court date. The "impossible" status was still intact, but this evening it was the possibilities that were most notable. This was a room full of joy and merriment with lots of laughter. The teddy bear received considerable attention as it was passed around the room, and kids and adults alike wound it up to hear the little bear play his tune again and again.

CHAPTER 8

Too Late?

NOW OUR DAYS WOULD BE very full, travelling to Cluj, some days with Lenuta and other days without. And so began the arduous process of wading through the pile of documents to be filled out, after which we would begin our interviews. We had to attend a series of meetings during which we would present our American paperwork. Even though we had been approved by American laws, we needed to also be approved by Romanian law. The big problem was getting all this done before the last court date. If we could not meet all of the requirements for court by that last date, our whole case would be thrown out. We had one shot at this process with a largely uncooperative system and many steps in which one official would have the power to stall the whole thing until it was too late.

It was a bright, sunny day for our first meeting in Cluj. With Cornell behind the wheel, we piled into the van and then picked up Lenuta for her part in the process. Once at the appointed government location in Cluj, we spent hours filling out paperwork and waiting on benches in hallways or chairs in offices for whatever meeting was next. During one of the waiting-on-benches period, I discovered something astounding. There is a language that can be heard through the heart. As we sat on the bench that day an entire conversation took place between Lenuta and I that was as real as if the most profound Romanian and the most eloquent English was being spoken aloud. As she looked straight into my eyes, suddenly I could almost hear her thoughts. She was saying something like this: "I am trusting you. I love my children, and I am sending them with you because I need to, not because I don't want them. I am trusting you to take care of them and raise them well." I have never forgotten that commission, and I took it seriously. I pledged in that moment that I would do my best to raise these children in a way that would make her proud of them and also that we would raise them to know and love God, to have friends and a happy, carefree childhood. Lenuta held my gaze and then smiled and nodded on cue, as if she had caught every word. I was stunned at the clarity despite the fact that our voices hadn't been needed, and language had come straight from the soul. We had made an agreement that day, more solid and powerful than any document lawyers and judges could draw up and enforce. I looked forward to the day when these children were grown and were loving, responsible, successful people. Then maybe we could come back, and Lenuta would meet them again and be proud.

We met with a series of people who each had to approve us before we were sent to the next. First was a lady behind a rather large desk. Once again Cornell was busy translating. As she turned her attention to Lenuta and glanced at the paperwork, her expression and tone became stern and disapproving, and they remained that way throughout the brief interview. I was struck how this lady could form such a judgment on so little as that piece of paper. How could she know the path Lenuta had traveled? It didn't seem to bother Lenuta, though, and we were approved. We next met with a woman who appeared to be about fifty years of age. She had dark hair, wore a blue shiny dress, and seemed to have lots of energy. She was bustling all over as we walked beside her, relaying our information as she went from one place to another. She stamped her approval, and on to the next place we went. We found ourselves in a large, stately room with very high ceilings and beautiful woodwork throughout. The grand room was furnished with a very large desk, a tall leather chair, and some artwork, which was unusual to see in these places. The man behind the desk was in his late forties with a moustache, a nice suit and this office to himself. It was a very nice surprise to have him greet us in English. He was pleasant but serious and took his time to review all the facts. When he had finished his fact-finding questions, he stood up from his desk and came and sat closer to us in a more personal manner. He began talking to Jon about various topics such as school and sports. He then remarked that he also had a son, who was younger than Jon. He commented that he thought it was wonderful that we had come here to adopt and that he and his wife were considering adopting as well.

We also had to get our American documents translated, which needed to be done by special lawyers. This was very time consuming, and so Cornell was constantly needing to monitor the progress. This was the tricky part, as the deadline was very near, and everything had to be one hundred percent completed properly and perfectly. From what we had been hearing, the American Embassy was operating the same way. Once the process was done on this end with the Romanian government, it all had to be cleared again on the American side as well. Apparently, many cases were being rejected because of incomplete or inaccurate paperwork and documentation. The following day was our court date, and the paperwork still was not ready. Finally, we were informed it would not be completed until morning. Once the translating was finally finished, we still had to pick the paperwork up from across town and take it to a different location where Lenuta, Brian, and I would sign in the presence of the notary.

We were able to pick up our completed paperwork fairly early in the morning, but still needed to get it notarized. We dashed across town. Once inside the building, we asked a woman if she could direct us toward the notary office. I'm sure she noticed our frantic dispositions because she offered to take us there herself. While hurrying toward our destination, we explained our mission and the time dilemma we were facing, and she immediately rallied to our cause. As we approached the office to take care of this last piece of the puzzle, it appeared as if all might be well and we would make it in time. That was until we actually arrived at the notary's location and there in the hallway was a line out the door and a mob standing there pressing forward trying to get in. It would take hours for this crowd to finish their business in the office, yet now minutes were all we had.

Our new friend told us to follow her as she pushed through the crowd and boldly up to the front. She faced her colleague who was busy notarizing at a small table and spoke to her in Romanian, pointing to us, our papers, and finally the clock. Apparently, the notary was neither amused nor sympathetic and spoke very angrily to our helper and to Cornell. Our new friend turned out to be quite spunky. She nodded politely to the notary agent, whirled around still smiling, and motioned for us to follow. She went at a fast clip and headed to another room where there was yet another notary agent with exactly the same situation going on—a line out the door and a crowd down the hall. Cornell, Brian, Jon, and Lenuta managed to get through the crowd and into the door, at which time it closed. The crowd edged closer to the door, and I simply could not get through. A few seconds later, the door opened and Cornell's head popped out. He spotted me, reached through the crowd, and pulled me through the doorway despite the protests from the people who were in line. This notary was entirely different and quickly checked our IDs, pointed out where to sign, and stamped where needed. We now had only minutes until our court time, and we still had to hurry across the building and up some flights of stairs to get to the courtroom. We thanked our helper and offered her some American money. A twenty-dollar bill would probably have equaled a month's salary at that time. I was astounded when she replied that she would not take our money because God would bless her for helping us and then motioned for us to go quickly.

We rushed down a long hallway and then up several flights of stairs as fast as we could. We finally arrived, a bit breathless, at the courtroom door, and we walked in to discover it was standing room only. We squeezed into a corner in the back as the doors we had just rushed through were officially closed. No more people would be allowed in. The atmosphere was tense and serious with hushed, nervous talking buzzing throughout as people watched the door in front where the judge and his assistants would enter the room. Finally, the door opened. Dressed in judge's robe with notebook in hand, the man who had interviewed us in the grand office the week before stepped up to the bench. When we had spoken to him, we had no idea he was a judge; we had just assumed he was the next person on our interview chain. Right behind the judge came the dark-haired friendly woman who had worn the blue shiny dress during our interview with her. As his assistant, she took the place by his side.

A few cases were heard, and when the room cleared a bit, we made our way to seats near the front. The judge's demeanor was not even slightly the same as it had been while we were in his office the week before when he had sat down to chat with Jon. He was serious, stern, and formidable, speaking harshly at times to defendants and attorneys before him. Finally, our names were called, and we all went up front. After we were sworn in, he asked questions in a very serious tone. He never acknowledged that he remembered us. Finally after what seemed like a very long moment in which he and his assistant looked over our paperwork, he pronounced that the adoption would be approved. He ordered a seventeen-day waiting period to give all parties time to reconsider. After the time was up, we would sign more documents confirming that our intentions had not changed, and then we would be free to go on to the next steps.

CHAPTER 9

Cluj-Napoca

WE HAD MUCH TO ACCOMPLISH during this two-and-a-half-week waiting period. We arranged with Lenuta that we would pick the children up in the mornings for outings. That way the children would get to know us in a gradual and pleasant process. Before our departure from home, we had sent ahead boxes of items. Now we began planning how to distribute these goods. It was actually very easy to place these items because there was so much need everywhere, and though we had lots, I wished we had more. Cornell's dad could distribute the Romanian Bibles that we had brought, so they went to him, and the medical supplies would go to the local hospital. There was a young lady in the village who had a toddler daughter and had just given birth to a baby girl. The family could find practically nothing at all in the stores to buy for their newborn. My mind flashed back to the stores at home with racks and racks of beautiful items. Villagers were happy to get the baby food, formula, diapers, and assorted-sized clothes. I saw the young mother in the village later with her baby wrapped in the pink blanket, bonnet, and booties we had brought, and her toddler was also dressed all pink and pretty beside her mom. They looked so adorable and bright against the contrast of the wet muddy street.

We delivered some medical supplies to the nearby hospital. The hospital did not look particularly clean or bright and certainly not cheerful in any regard. There were no plants or artwork, and everything seemed dim and dingy. Of course, the lighting in Romanian buildings was never good due to the lack of fixtures and light bulbs; unfortunately even the hospitals were dealing with these shortages. There was a lack of proper supplies and equipment, one of them being syringes, which were being used over and over, sometimes not getting proper sterilization because of power outages. In the village, I had visited with a young mother who had recently given birth via Caesarian section. She lifted up her blouse to show me her scar, which was a shocking sight. It was the length of her abdomen and quite wide. It looked as if she had been hacked by a huge knife. It was healing fine, thankfully, but I wondered how many new mothers did not survive such a surgery.

We also went to visit Cornell's aunt and uncle at their home a short way outside the village. After enjoying their hospitality and a hot cup of tea at the table, we all took a walk outside on their property. It was a nice time for Cornell and his uncle to visit a bit, and Cornell once again was valiant at keeping us in the loop as to what they were discussing. At one point, Cornell explained to us that, years ago, a tree had fallen on his uncle's head. As if this wasn't shocking enough Cornell asked his uncle to take off his hat. On the top right side of his head was a deep dent the size and shape of a log. How he ever survived is a mystery to me.

Several mornings during this waiting period, Cornell, Brian, Jon, and I picked the children up in Cornell's car for the outings. This was big excitement for the kids because riding in a car and going outside their little community was new, and they were always full of anticipation. There was plenty of conversation among kids and adults alike throughout the village concerning Mariora and Gaby going to America, which made them a bit like celebrities. They seemed to enjoy this whole experience and especially driving away in the car through their neighborhood for another exciting escapade. We went many places, and one favorite was a piece of property Cornell's family owned which was on a beautiful little creek. The "boys" would engage in a spirited soccer match. It was always America against Romania with Brian, Jon, and Cornell against three other friends or relatives of

Cornell. The kids would be the ball chasers, and when it was kicked out of bounds, they would run to the fence, be swung over it by the nearest competitor, and dash off after it. Then they would return with the ball and be swung back over the fence. It amazed me how the Romanian guys would play barefoot.

Then there was a big Romanian barbeque to top it off. The barbeque equipment was much different than ours. It consisted of a big metal bowl with a metal rod through the center. The bowl was suspended over the ground, and a fire was built underneath. The bowl was filled with lard or some kind of fat, which was heated until it was very hot. Meat and potatoes were thrown in and sizzled away until done. We always had plenty of food while we were visiting, even though, just several years prior to that time during the communist years, there had been an extreme shortage. The circumstances were not much better, and in some ways, they were worse because switching to a market economy is a difficult process. The bread lines were still very long, and people could wait for hours and then end up with nothing. There were also milk lines, which were similar.

The meat served to us by the villagers was usually pork, chicken, or lamb they had raised themselves, and we had vegetables from their gardens. We were very surprised one evening when we opened the closet door in the room we were staying in and found a dead pig hanging there. That part of the house no doubt had the coolest temperature since there was no refrigeration in the village. Pieces would be cut off the carcass for the next meal, and the leftover meat was saved and recooked the following day. As guests, we were always served the freshest and best. We did have to be careful of the water, though, but we were able to get bottles of "appa mineral"—bottled mineral water—that was a life saver for us.

We took the kids to various places in Cluj. We went to a park and played on the swings and the slide, and we went to an open market where villagers sold their vegetables, flowers, and fruit. We even found someone selling ice cream. The kids enjoyed their first ice cream, which resulted in their feeling even more favorable toward the prospect of going to America, the land of teddy bears, ice cream, chocolate and

40

bomboanes—candy. Gaby, being three and not accustomed to markets, was mesmerized by a pile of cherries that an older man was selling. He began helping himself, loading his pants pockets and shirt pocket with the cherries. This was a treat the kids didn't often get, and he could not resist. The man was very kind and smiled and laughed, even though these cherries were valuable to him, as they were all he was selling that day. We, of course, paid the man for his cherries and knew the lesson of buying and selling would be one taught at another time, somewhere down the road that lay ahead of us all.

We enjoyed observing many of the differences of life here in Romania. One of these still makes me laugh. Early each morning a certain person, whose job it was, would pick up the cows from their individual homes and take them out to graze in the pastures. After the cows spent the day feasting in the lush, green pastures on a nearby knoll, the cow herder would return them home, walking behind as they meandered their way through the neighborhood streets. The herder might have been unnecessary, however, as these cute cows knew exactly where their own places were. The families would leave their gates open when it was nearing the time for the cows to return. As each cow came to its home, it would veer off into the entrance without any prompting, knowing full well its own street, gate, and home. There was no cause to worry if someone neglected to open the gate, however. The cow would simply moo loudly and somewhat impatiently until its remiss owner would rush over to let it in. When the gate was finally opened, the cow would hurry in, appearing very happy to be back after such a hard day of dining on the hill.

The women in the village washed their clothes in small washtubs after first drawing the water from a well and heating it on the wood stove. They would scrub and wring out each item by hand. Some days they would haul their laundry to the river to wash it, and on very frozen winter days, they would break the ice and wash the clothes in the freezing water. The clothes were then hung on lines strung outside on sunny days or strung through their living rooms during inclement weather. There were no coffee shops or movie theaters. There weren't even any phones. To place a call, we had to take the half-hour drive to

Cluj and go to a telephone center. It was a large room lined with phones hanging on the wall, benches for waiting your turn, and a counter in front. Behind the counter were several phone operators with headsets like those used in the early days of phones. After waiting our turn at the counter, we would give the receptionist the phone number we wished to call. She, in turn, would assign us to a phone. Once we stationed ourselves at the correct phone and lifted the receiver, she would connect our call. Of course, it was expensive, so most people could not afford to use these phones.

Lisa, Mariora, Gaby, and Lenuta in
Somesu Rece, Romania, 1991.

Mariora on one of our hikes up into the
hills of Somesu Rece, Romania.

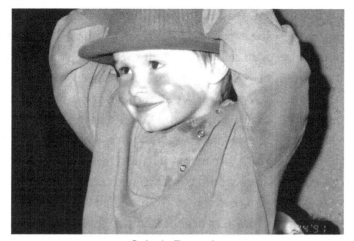

Gaby in Romania.

Jon experiencing sibling life in our rental
house in Cluj-Napoca, Romania.

The Somesu Rece villagers were very hospitable and were continually inviting us to dinner. After we returned from an overnight trip to some hot springs, one of our invitations came from Lenuta. It was an all-day project that involved catching and beheading several chickens, plucking, gutting, and cutting them up, and finally frying them over the wood stove. We were looking forward to spending time with the kids and Lenuta in their home. Lenuta was a gracious hostess, and the chicken, which she served with a cucumber and tomato salad fresh from her garden, was very tasty and also fresh since it all had been living in the yard earlier that day. Lenuta's husband, Gheorghe, talked continually, even though Cornell spent little time translating, and finally Gheorghe said he thought we wanted to take his son, Lenuta's third child, to America. We assured him that was not the case, though the child was very darling, and I would have loved to take him too but, of course, this was never a possibility. The evening was fun, even though Gheorghe was causing us all to feel a bit uncomfortable as we wondered what he would come up with next.

A few days later, we received word there had arisen complications and further drama from Gheorghe. Lenuta, through tears, relayed the newest developments. Gheorghe was now threatening to hide Gaby, thus preventing him from going with us. Gheorghe's objective, according to Lenuta, was that he would rather keep Gaby and put him to work as he grew older and stronger, as his worker or "slave" as she put it. Lenuta also knew the danger would never really be off the table of Gheorghe selling Gaby to black-market agents. She was feeling as though this opportunity of happiness for her children was crumbling before her eyes. It was a very sobering and dangerous turn of events, and we had been warned by villagers and Lenuta many times to take Gheorghe's threats seriously. We needed to take quick action, and so we devised a plan.

CHAPTER 10

Outsmarting Gheorghe

THE PLAN WE FORMULATED, WITH Lenuta's help, involved us picking the kids up early the following day, for an "ice cream" treat in Cluj and then, quite simply, never bringing them back. We would take them to a house in the city we had rented, and then spend the next several days organizing our documentation for the American Embassy, legally wrapping things up in Cluj, and finally arranging last-minute farewell meetings in parks or homes with Lenuta and other family members, excluding Gheorghe of course. It was a tense time, and Lenuta was worried, so we arrived early the next day and hoped Gheorghe had not suspected that we had been hatching a scheme. Unfortunately, Gheorghe could not be underestimated, and when we arrived, Lenuta was once again in tears, and Gaby was nowhere to be found.

Gheorghe had whisked himself and Gaby off very early, unbeknownst to Lenuta. But neither were we to be underestimated. We were resolved to wait for Gaby's return or search until we found him and put an end to Gheorghe's tiresome tactics once and for all. Having no allies in the village to turn to for help, Gheorghe was on his own. He finally showed up, hoping we had already picked up Mariora and left. He had given firm instructions to Gaby not to allow us to take him. When Gheorghe and Gaby walked through the gate,

Gaby saw us. Following his instruction from Gheorghe, he ran over to their chained dog, which was barking in a rabid manner. Trained to be watch dogs, many of these Romanian canines were tied and vicious, pulling frantically and wildly at their ropes, growling and barking with teeth bared, and threatening to tear any person within reach into pieces. They were quite frightening and intimidating, so Gheorghe's plan could have worked had this particular dog been larger than approximately ten pounds. Gaby, being three, quickly grew tired of standing next to the snarling little dog and getting nipped at himself, so he left his post and wandered over to see what we were up to, knowing it was usually ice cream or some other fun. We were able to convince Gheorghe that we were going for ice cream as we had many times before. He looked skeptical but finally believed it to be true, so we quickly loaded the kids in the car, knowing they would not be back. And we didn't feel entirely safe until the car started up and took off out of the village for good. And, for the record, we did actually get ice cream.

The kids settled in quickly and easily into our temporary home in Cluj, and most of all loved playing with the water coming out of the faucet in the bathroom. They had not seen running water before and laughed with delight as they put their finger in the stream and pulled it out, repeating this again and again. High on their "to do" list also was playing with Jon. They climbed on him continuously, playing games with the balls that were left at the house, and running in the small yard outside. They also enjoyed watching playback videos of themselves on the camcorder, and Jon was very patient turning it on and holding it for them as they watched and laughed. They were not so enthusiastic about bath time, though. Each of them cried when presented with the idea of getting into the nice warm water that barely filled the tub. Cornell, who was always coming to the rescue, did so once again, explaining in Romanian to the kids how wonderful a nice warm bath could be. Soon they were giggling and drenching the bathroom with their exuberant splashes of soapy water.

Brian and I agreed we would make some name changes for the kids that we felt might fit better in America. The English translation for Mariora was Maria or Mary, and since I had always loved the name Mary, we decided this would be it. We kept her beautiful Romanian middle name, Rozalia, as a connection to her heritage. Gaby is a nickname for his given name, Gavrel, which translated to English is Gabriel. Since he had only one name, we put Michael as his first name and Gabriel as his middle name. Now he was named after not one, but two, archangels from the Bible, so we thought we were pretty clever and were happy with our decisions.

Our last visit to the village was with Rodica's family. We all went outdoors to enjoy the clear, warm spring day complete with a sprinkling of puffy clouds against the blue sky. We picnicked at a table in the yard under a beautiful sprawling tree, and I was taking in these last moments in the village and still felt as if I had been transported into a book of some sort—like a novel set a hundred years ago. I could see a short way into the distance Rodica's sister going to the family well and drawing water. The late afternoon sun made the picturesque scene appear like a dream with the beautiful young lady in her dress and apron drawing water by lowering the bucket, carefully cranking it up, and then carrying her bucket back to the house again. It was customary that the women did not sit down to eat with the guests, and no matter how much coaxing they received from us, it simply wasn't done. They would not join us, but happily attended the table trying to refill our plates and our water glasses as much as we would let them.

After dinner, we relaxed and visited with the family and Lenuta. There was a short game of Romania verses America soccer played with Rodica's young brothers. Our last time with Lenuta was pleasant, but at last her tears were flowing. She remained throughout the whole sequence from beginning to end a loving and courageous mother and woman. I will always have respect for her as we witnessed her fight, heard from the villagers of her many prayers, and watched her prevail through faith and determination in the effort to get her endangered children to safety. She was careful to hide her tears and these parting emotions from the children and was pleasant and positive while near them. We finally said our last goodbyes, and David took us to the train station in Cluj.

We stood outside the train station with our luggage beside us and tickets in hand, gazing down the tracks waiting for our train to appear. We hung on tightly to the children's hands and finally caught a glimpse of the locomotive chugging our direction. I had a gloomy feeling, and a cold shudder went down my spine as we saw it approaching. Here again, I suddenly felt dropped into the pages of a history book or a scene from a movie as I saw an old-model steam engine approach. This station did have an eerie similarity to the train stations depicted in World War Two movies. When the train came into view, I could see the similarity to the trains that had transported prisoners to concentration camps during that horrible era. The steam engines at that time in history would also be pulling many box cars into which so many unwilling passengers had been shoved. My mind went back to historical events long past, to a terrible nightmarish time, and I wanted to shake the images out of my head that were beginning to come alive—flashes of mothers, fathers, babies, and grandparents pushed into the train to begin a journey toward doom. I was glad when the kids started jumping with excitement and I was jolted back to the present. We stepped onto the train and found our places in the sleeper car section.

We all slept surprisingly well, although we were startled awake on few occasions by a horn blast or some other noise. We would always find Mary still sitting up wide awake and intently gazing at the countryside now far beyond her village. The trip to the train car bathroom was an experience in itself, for upon entering I saw a perfectly normal-looking toilet and sink. "Normal" stopped soon after I lifted the toilet lid only to discover an amazingly clear view of the train tracks racing by below. There was no running water from the sink faucet either. We doubled up on taking the kids because that hole to the tracks seemed frighteningly large to me, and I felt better with someone else hanging onto the kids too.

CHAPTER 11

Bucharest: Final Hurdles

AT LAST THE SUN AROSE, and a beautiful morning dawned as the train came to a slow, grinding halt at the Bucharest train station. We had been warned even before leaving the United States that Bucharest was full of turmoil. There was an uprising of the Romani population. Not to be confused with Romanians, the Romani people, known by others as "gypsies," also found themselves in the post-revolutionary chaos. There was also a corrupt and powerful black market dealing in goods and currency. This information had been front-page news right before we left home, and our parents had warned us to be very careful. It seemed we could sense a heavy oppression in the air, even though a gorgeous spring morning was doing its best to present itself. We could see lots of bullet holes in buildings. There were tables with embroidered table cloths topped with burning candles lined up along the sidewalks with fresh, young faces smiling back from framed photos, portraying those who had been shot and died in these very spots.

As the government collapsed, the rise of the criminal element had quickly and tenaciously grabbed a foothold. These black-market dealers traded in children, currency exchange, and stealing, all through violence and intimidation. Yet there was also a determination in the air that this corruption would not prevail. I continued to take in these

49

disturbing sights as we walked by the bullet-riddled buildings which were still not repaired a year and a half after the destruction. We took a taxi and arrived at our hotel, which looked as though it had been grand at one point in time. It was also full of bullet holes. The lobby looked nice, and the clerk was friendly. He gave us our keys, and we went to our rooms, which were on the sixth floor. Our rooms were equipped with old-model televisions, working bathrooms, beds, and dressers. We all decided to watch a movie in our room and noticed there were no news channels and even on the radio station no world news was broadcast. The only news we received through the media was that it was President George H. Bush's birthday, even though much was going on in the Middle East with the Persian Gulf War recently ending and uprisings in Iraq springing up. A Phil Collins concert came on, which was lots of fun, and some movies were on next. The movies were usually French or German with Romanian subtitles so we were out of luck until an American or English movie was shown. An old Elizabeth Taylor, Spencer Tracy movie came on called "Father's Little Dividend" and we enjoyed it even though it was made about forty years before.

We were fairly rested, so we decided to eat in the hotel restaurant. We then walked a few blocks to a huge park where the kids could run around and have some fun and use up a bit of the energy they had previously been using by climbing onto the television console, jumping on and off the beds, flushing and re-flushing the toilet, and splashing in the water stream coming from the faucet.

In the morning, we went to the hotel restaurant for breakfast. The food was good, but immediately we encountered problems. Some rather large men were loitering around the lobby and staring at the hotel guests. For some reason, they seemed to zero in on us. When we finished our meal, we headed toward the lobby. Two of the men came up to us and started talking loudly. They were exhibiting extremely pushy behavior, holding out Romanian currency and saying, "Change money. Change money!" This did not sound like a request at all, but rather a demand. We had been warned never to exchange money with strangers, as many were crooks and would fold bills in such a way and with sleight of hand in order to rip the victims off most every time. They would then accuse the victim of deceiving them and the fight would be on.

Brian was a bit weary with constantly being asked to change money, and he tried to firmly decline so they would stop bothering us. Several of the large, burly guys got right into his face just as Cornell walked into the lobby. One big guy went straight up to Cornell with a small spray bottle pointed right in his eye. He accused Cornell of selling the kids to us. Cornell didn't even blink. He looked straight at the guy, denied it, and then went on to say it wasn't the guy's business what we were doing. The standoff lasted a few more seconds, and then they left. But we knew we were not welcome in their area unless we did business with them. I began to have doubts about having brought Jon on this trip. The village and Cluj seemed safe, but Bucharest was feeling very dangerous.

The next day our trip to the American Embassy was scheduled, and we hoped this process would be speedy and successful. Rodica's brother, Grigore, was to join us the following day and accompany us to the embassy. He was attempting to obtain a work visa and come to the United States, as many Romanians wished to do. We were optimistic, primarily because he was Cornell's brother-in law. As US citizens, we could perhaps vouch for him too, which, between these two possibilities, could potentially tip the decision in his favor.

Bright and early the next morning, we all hopped into a taxi; we were to meet Grigore in front of the embassy. The taxi ride was frightening as there seemed to be no laws whatsoever on speed, whether the driver drove on sidewalks, or which side they passed oncoming automobiles on—the sidewalk side or the oncoming traffic side. All the while they wove wildly in and out of tight spots going way too fast. I was not sure who to be most afraid of, our cab driver or the others participating in the same driving style. Pedestrians had no right of way, and many of them were dodging traffic that did not make the slightest effort to slow down for them. It was shocking indeed seeing so many near misses, and I was relieved to exit the taxi at our destination while each of us was still in one piece.

We could not get near the gate to the embassy as there were hordes of people waving American flags trying for a chance to get in. They had cardboard cutouts on sticks depicting the statue of liberty and signs that read "Washington says yes but Bucharest says no." This referred to the fact that the words on the Statue of Liberty invite them there, but the Americans in the embassy refuse them. There were armed marines and high fences to keep the mob of people at bay. It was startling on so many levels and gave us a new thankfulness for being born into a free nation such as ours. The people didn't understand that many thousands of Romanians immigrate to America, but the embassy couldn't let everyone in without going through the legal process.

We held up our US passports, which at that moment seemed like pure gold to me, and the marine closest to us looked alarmed and made the crowd part so we could approach. They scrutinized our passports, and then let us through. We entered the large area where there were smaller waiting areas and lines. Grigore had to line up in a separate area. He had all his paperwork in order, except for his signature at the bottom. He checked it all over, borrowed a pen, signed his name, and then waited nervously in line. When at last his turn came, there was a small commotion as the agent checked over his paperwork and quickly denied his application. Cornell was nearby and joined Grigore at the window to hear from the agent regarding the basis for this rejection. The agent explained that, because two different colors of ink had been used—one color to fill it out and another to sign his name—the application would not be accepted because it appeared that it could possibly have been stolen or forged. No amount of pleading or protesting would change the outcome that day. That decision changed Grigore's path forever. He never did move to the United States.

Soon it was our turn to face the embassy representatives. They checked our paperwork meticulously but, surprisingly, we soon heard the sound of stamping as pages and pages of our paperwork were being approved. We had gone the extra mile, literally, by foot, bus, taxi, and automobile to interviews, attorneys' offices, and to legal translators and had gone through every instruction carefully and thoroughly.

There we stood with approved documents from the Romanian court system and the US Embassy. We were pleased and jubilant even though our work was still not over. Having received visas for the kids, we next had to get passports, but that evening we would celebrate with a nice dinner and begin again in the morning to secure the passports and plane tickets.

We were ready for a nice meal, and Cornell knew where we could get the best. Drawback? It was only for active Romanian military officers and their families. Growing up in that environment, Cornell learned at a young age how to talk a person into doing what ordinarily could not be done. Cornell was persuasive in his communication with the officer manning the door, and the next thing we knew we were being shown to our table. We were seated very near to a high-ranking officer who was dining alone. This made me slightly uncomfortable, as he was close enough to hear our every word. Michael quickly engaged him in conversation and asked if he had kids. The officer replied that he did, a daughter. Michael inquired as to her whereabouts, and the officer responded that she was at home and couldn't come with him. A perplexed, thoughtful expression crossed Michael's face as his three-year-old mind was processing this information. "What's the matter? Doesn't she have any legs?" Cornell and the officer laughed at this exchange, and then Cornell translated the conversation to us. Oh, but the fun was not over. The waiter approached our table to take our order, and as soon as Michael realized what he was doing, he quickly put in his order. For a beer. Michael proceeded to ask the waiter to show him his wrist watch. The waiter extended his wrist toward Michael. He was sporting a gold and possibly expensive timepiece. Michael was not impressed. He flung his own wrist in the waiter's direction to show off his very own orange plastic watch. The waiter complimented him on his watch, to which Michael replied that his orange watch was better than the waiter's. Oh dear. Of course, Michael did not get his beer, and I was making more mental notes of changes to come.

We had a quick breakfast the next morning in our hotel and noticed the same burly men loitering around and staring at us. We successfully ignored them but grew more alarmed at their intimidating attention. We headed off to the post office to get the kids' Romanian passports so they could travel, which included filling out paperwork and getting their pictures taken. The kids were not enjoying any of it, even though Cornell was explaining what we were doing. Fortunately, it was quickly done but with the menacing men in the lobby that morning, the gloomy weather, and the kids being a bit fussy, it did not feel like the day was getting off to a good start. Then we could hear the words *"Jos cu Iliescu. Jos cu Iliescu!"* loudly and angrily chanted by a number of people in unison. More people were joining in as the gathering rapidly increased in numbers. The chanting intensified. Suddenly we noticed some of the men trying to tip over a parked police car. Then, there it was, lying on its side in the road. We asked Cornell for an explanation. What did "jos cu Iliescu" mean? The interpretation was "Down with Iliescu." Ion Iliescu was the current president who had immediately followed Ceausescu after the revolution. Cornell further explained that Iliescu was not popular because the people felt he was supporting more of the same kind of government.

We barely had time to process the information before there were loud screams and many people began running in our direction, away from something. We looked back up the street and quickly grabbed the kids. We started running away in the midst of the fleeing crowd. We were jostled around a bit as people were bumping into each other in the effort to make a quick getaway. We ran down sidewalks and stairs, with the crowd finally scattering in different directions, yet we did not slow down until we felt we were a safe distance from what was coming. What we had witnessed were soldiers. They advanced in several rows that spanned the width of the street. They were fully dressed in uniforms, boots, and blue helmets. They carried guns and also batons for the purpose of striking those who displayed noncompliance. They were marching our direction to put a halt to what they considered an unruly and unlawful assembly. This was a scene that had played out many times in Romania over the years of communism—soldiers marching down streets beating people and shooting into crowds. We had heard about it before, and now we were seeing it. As one lady ran past us, she yelled for us to run faster. "They will beat you all!" she shouted.

Finally back in our hotel, we adults rested for a bit in our rooms while the children napped before we went down to a meal. The dining experience was engaging, with a singer and violinist playing to us at our table before they continued around the room to other tables. He was then accompanied by additional violinists. Together they played several American tunes including "Yankee Doodle," "The Star-Spangled Banner," and "America the Beautiful." It was all very enjoyable until we saw our black-market thugs staring at us from the lobby while they gave us the finger. We finally decided to complain to the hotel management. We found the manager to be gracious and apologetic enough; however, he explained that there was nothing that could be done about the situation. This was their "area," and even the police were afraid of them. This gang of black marketers would threaten the police and their families with violence if they dared to mess with their "territory." We had no choice but to relocate. Even the mentioning of this option to our hotel manager did not change a thing. He was powerless to offer a harassment-free visit for our time in his building, and so, after dinner, we packed up and moved to another hotel. It was a matter of personal safety. We knew they were dangerous, and we knew we were squarely in their sites.

CHAPTER 12

Flight West

OUR FLIGHT WITH TAROM AIRLINES was scheduled for eleven o'clock in the morning, and we arrived at the airport at around ten to allow enough time to get through the gates. We didn't want to rush the kids. Eleven o'clock quickly came, and we realized there was no plane anywhere in sight. Noon, one o'clock, and finally two o'clock came, and still there was no airplane on the tarmac. None of the personnel seemed to have any idea what was going on, where our plane was, when it would show up, or what time it could take off. We had not packed any food since we had planned to eat our lunch and then dinner while in flight. Unfortunately, neither did the airport have anything to eat. Finally, at four o'clock, as still there was not an airplane in sight, or a morsel of food, we rallied some other waiting passengers, which wasn't hard to do, and decided to approach an official in a more persuasive manner by forming a mob of sorts. This time we had a little more success, and finally we were told they would open the restaurant especially for us. Furthermore, they informed us that the plane would be there soon.

When we got to the dining area, the servers first brought us orange sugary drinks, which made me thirstier because of the high sugar content. Next came the plates of food. Every plate was identical to the other—two sandwiches, each one smaller than a quarter of a normal sandwich, and a very small serving of salad. It all quickly disappeared. Just as we were ready to request seconds, the announcement came that our plane had arrived and we must hurry to our gate as takeoff was imminent. After running down to the gate, we were talking excitedly among ourselves when someone had the presence of mind to look out the window, only to notice that there was still no airplane anywhere in sight. It was now about five o'clock. Still hungry, we all hurried back to the restaurant only to find the doors locked and no personnel anywhere nearby. It slowly dawned on us that the announcement of our flight arrival had been a ploy to get us out of the restaurant before we could request more food.

Two more hours went by and finally, the plane arrived. This next event, and apparently an airline custom with Tarom, was completely new to us. Since each passenger possessed a ticket but no seat assignment, it was a mad dash race to the plane where shoving and pushing were allowed and necessary. Cornell had warned us about this just before we got off the bus that took us across to the plane, so we were ready to fight our way to victory with the best of them. The prize was a seat, hopefully next to other members of our party, but negotiations between passengers could potentially get us closer to our party members. Cornell and Brian each carried a child as we exited the bus. We ran our hearts out across the pavement, up the stairs, and into the plane to claim our seats. We were each able to secure a spot, and Cornell began negotiations with other seat claimants, and so we ended up fairly near each other.

Our first stop over was a quick one in Amsterdam. How exciting it was to touch the ground in a free-market economy in a thriving country. We had the opportunity to leave the aircraft, possibly buy some snacks, stretch our legs, and use the restrooms. I will never forget the moment I stepped out of the plane, walked across the exit ramp, and entered the airport. We were greeted at the gate by a well-dressed, perfectly groomed young woman employee who welcomed us to Amsterdam in the English language as she shook the hand of each person who exited the plane and entered her country. She seemed to know who spoke what language and changed her greeting accordingly. The airport was spotlessly clean and decorated with beautiful plants and artwork. It was a fully modernized, state-of-the art facility. Brian and Jon took Michael to the men's room while Mary and I entered the ladies'. We were impressed by the extraordinarily clean and fully functioning bathroom with bright lights and sparkling fixtures. As we were stepping into a stall, Mary laughed when a tissue toilet seat cover mechanically came from somewhere and covered the seat. When we were finished, the toilet flushed itself and took the seat cover along. At the sink, the soap dispensed its froth into our hands and the faucet turned on and off at the appropriate intervals. Oh, what a change a flight can make. Mary giggled with surprise and delight at this restroom's astounding performance. What I was unaware of then was that, in our future, another plane ride—a flight east—would transform our lives once again.

PART
FOUR

Welcome
to America

The best thing about the future is that
it comes one day at a time.
~Abraham Lincoln

CHAPTER 13

Settling In

WE ARRIVED IN NEW YORK and had a short stay in a hotel. We made it to the buffet breakfast before the shuttle arrived to take us back to the airport. If I were to go back to that buffet, these many years later, I might not be so impressed, but that morning it looked like the most amazing display of breakfast items ever. There was an array of fresh fruit, eggs, bacon, biscuits, sweet rolls, yogurt, and more. The kids were wide-eyed but mannerly as they helped themselves and made several trips back to choose more from the scrumptious feast beautifully spread out before us. I felt gratefulness and delight for all the road blocks that had been overcome to make this new life possible. I recalled how God had spoken to me in this very city when we were ready to board our connecting flight overseas and ultimately into Bucharest. He assured me that He would be working on our behalf, in spite of my concerns and shortcomings. And indeed He had.

Challenging days were certain to be upon us as we prepared to raise children who, for now, did not understand our words; neither did we understand theirs. Mary seemed to have a grasp of the concept of different languages, but many times, while still in Romania, Michael would look at us as if we were completely incompetent and maybe even stupid. After all, we appeared to have no idea how to make any sense when speaking, forcing Cornell to explain to anyone nearby what we were trying to say with our garbled nonsensical speech. We arrived home to our little condo across from the beach. Before leaving for Romania, I had put away the pretty bedspread and some breakable items because we were going to have some renovating done while we were gone. The work had never been done, and our little home was not looking its best as we burst through its front door, but it appeared like a palace to me. Friends and family who knew we were bringing home two new family members had stocked our refrigerator, brought in mattresses, and made beds for the kids. Near the beds were piles of wrapped presents in colorful children's gift wrap and ribbons. We had such a fun evening while the kids opened presents while snacking on graham crackers, milk, and fresh fruit.

Cornell was home with Rodica, and we were on our own to navigate through these transitions. We found that communicating with the children was much easier than we imagined using pointing, nodding, head shakes, frowns, and smiles mixed in with simple words from both languages. It was mostly nonverbal at the beginning, so the communication in our family evolved into skits, hand motions, funny faces, and lots of pointing. It was like the game of charades. We soon began introducing more and more English words, and Jon helped turn it into a game, having them repeat after us, which the kids participated in with enthusiasm. We had an English/Romanian dictionary, but in Michael's case especially, it proved mostly useless. It didn't include an English/Romanian baby talk section, so we were out of luck there. He pronounced the sound "f" with a "sh" sound so the word *frig*, which means "cold" in Romanian, he pronounced "shig". Also, the word for "hot" in Romanian is *cald*, which of course sounds like "cold," so this added confusion and complicated matters. However, in spite of these issues, we were all learning rather quickly as we spanned the gap of the communication barrier.

The summer was an adventure. It proved to be a beautiful one with many sunny days and lots of strawberries, cherries, and ice cream. We visited family members and made many trips to the beach across the street. The evenings were fun with car rides, local outdoor events, picnics, and barbeques. The kids always liked to stop at the nearby supermarket and put a quarter into the slot on the smiling plastic horse by the front door. They would ride as if they were on the fastest, wildest horse alive. When we went into the grocery store, the kids could not contain themselves and would point and squeal with delight over the abundance, especially at the rows of fresh fruit and vegetables. Fresh fruit was scarce in Romania, and mostly what they had available was grown themselves. We did buy fruit each time, of course, and when they kept pointing at different kinds, I would have to tell them "no," as we could only eat so much fruit before it spoiled. Not being able to explain all these details to them, I would let them pick out a few kinds, and to the rest of their pointing I would say "not today." In response, and being agreeable, they would proceed around the produce aisle pointing at each item proclaiming in loud high-pitched excited voices, "Not today. Not today." Fellow customers smiled at the cute and happy kids but did have slightly perplexed expressions at such exuberance over fruit and vegetables.

The evening car rides were interesting. Mary and Michael would sit in the back seat chatting to each other in Romanian. We heard our names quite often, and both kids would be glancing back and forth at us as they were discussing Daddy, Mommy, and Jonny. As time went by and they had learned enough English, I finally could ask them what they had been saying in Romanian on those summer evening drives. Apparently, they had been discussing who they liked best— Daddy, Mommy, or Jonny. The unanimous consensus was Jonny, and it sounded as if it was by a long shot.

We decided it was never too early to begin the children on small simple chores. Jon had started young, and so had developed a habit of helping. It was part of being a family. Mary would dust a couple of living room end tables and the coffee table while Michael was intrigued with putting on some rubber gloves, sprinkling a little Comet Cleanser in the bathroom sink, scrubbing it with his sponge, and rinsing it all away. They cooperated very nicely and were eager to help. Michael especially loved his job, and was very upset when, one bleak day, we were out of Comet. It was a double disaster, as we were out of lettuce as well, one of Michael's favorites. I wasn't exactly getting why he loved iceberg lettuce so much, but possibly it was the drama of tearing the leaves off the head and stuffing them into his mouth and crunch, crunch, crunching away. He did it with such gusto, and he could finish off a head in record time.

Going to the store was an enjoyable experience for the kids. Mary would grab the plastic kid-sized grocery cart and "shop" away moving through the aisles at a rate that was hard to keep up with while trying to shop myself. One day it was not going well, and soon we were separated. I was racing around looking for her when I spotted her up by the register saying *"Unde* Mommy?" to the clerk, which meant "Where is Mommy?" in Romanian. I actually think she needed me only so that I would produce the funds to pay for her "shopping." On another one of our supermarket runs, after learning some English, Michael was sitting in the seat of the cart and was begging me in a loud, pleading voice to please, *please* buy Comet and lettuce. I added these items to my cart quickly so that the high-volume requests would stop. Although now, as we paraded throughout the store, Michael was profusely thanking me for buying lettuce and Comet, again on high volume.

Our trips to and from the stores and our daily outings were full of attempts at communication, and the kids were definitely picking up English words. Mary learned to say "Today?" and it was always said with a question mark inflexion on the last syllable meaning what are we doing today? Then "Tomorrow?" Then it was "Next?" which meant what are we doing the day after, and she would then want to know the schedule for the entire week including what we were having for each meal. After I would tell her she would say "And?" which meant what's after that? I have never been much of a planner, but apparently, the little Romanian cutie pie sitting next to me came complete with a planner-style personality.

Our families were delighted when we brought home the two adorable new family members. When we were preparing to go to Romania, our parents were worried for our safety and the complications and expenses we might encounter through taking on the task of adopting. But all this changed in an instant as they met Mary and Michael for the first time. Brian's dad, Bill Bate, took a special interest and wanted them to come over often and play in the yard while Brian's mom, Dorothy, made lunches and dinners for all of us. One evening we were seated at Bill and Dorothy's dining room table. Bill stood up from his chair at the head of the table and asked for everyone's attention. He said he wanted to say a prayer, which was not his usual beginning to a family meal, but this time was different. He prayed most eloquently, thanking God for bringing Mary and Michael into our family. He said that, from that time on, they were just as important and equal as any member of the family. Then he ceremoniously walked over to the coffee table, retrieved the oversized family Bible, opened it, and added their names. Of all the people who expressed concern at the onset of our idea, Bill was the one who had seemed most agitated and uncertain, trying to change our minds until the last time we saw him before boarding the airplane to Romania.

It was not all pretty adjusting to our new roles within the family. Mary has remarkable leadership qualities and began, upon arriving home from Romania, to take her place as the head of the house. She loved to give us all directives in her broken English with a tone of great authority. It didn't fly with any of the family members, and so she was relegated back to the five-year-old daughter spot again after a good try. Her management skills would have to be perfected for use in the far future. The kids in the area loved to play with Mary and Michael, and they showered them with lots of attention. They were intrigued by the Romanian language and would ask them to talk. Then they would argue among themselves as to who got to push them on the swings next. Mary would repeat a phrase over and over during these times, and they would all gather around thinking it was so very cute. They wanted the kids to talk more. It seemed cute to me too, imagining she was saying something like "push me again," and I was glad to see how well everything was going. That is, until we asked Cornell, when we saw him next, what the phrase meant. He said it meant "leave me alone."

Jon was great fun and took on the role of "big brother extraordinaire" quickly and easily. He played with the kids, helped them pronounce words properly, and had special ways of engaging them, especially in the car during family outings. At times when the car was stopped, he would point to the ceiling light and say he could turn it on without touching it. Mary and Michael would shout that he could not, and subsequently Jon made a big dramatic show of it, opening his hands so the kids could see they were empty of any device, waving his hands, motioning to the light to obey, at which moment the light would suddenly come on. Now, the secret to this trick was that he had the door ajar ever so slightly, and when he subtly leaned in to it, the door would open further, causing the light to switch on. At the intersections with traffic lights, Jon would announce that he could turn these lights as well. He would drag out the whole thing until he could tell, by the order of the lights changing in the other lanes of traffic, when our light would be turning. The wide-eyed kids were completely impressed. As the kids got older, Jon helped them with homework, sports, and even helped Mary learn to dance before a prom. He was a big part of this whole endeavor, and we appreciated it enormously, especially his help with their homework—in particular, the math.

On one ordinary cleaning day, I found a scattered pile of loose chocolate chips thrown behind the living room couch. Obviously, they had been abandoned in haste as someone, most likely Mommy, was entering the room unexpectedly, and the culprit, having no time to enjoy the snack, aborted the operation abruptly. Finding the children playing in the bedroom and upon interrogation, Mary looked me in the eye and said, "Mommy, it was not me. I didn't do it." Michael, who would not lift his gaze from the carpet, stuttered and stammered, hemmed and hawed, and said it wasn't him. By their responses I pronounced the obvious verdict. "Michael, it was you. Now go clean it up." As I walked out the door I could hear the conversation between them as Michael asked Mary how Mommy knew it was him. They were both astounded and impressed at my unexplainable wisdom. It made me laugh, and I knew that, all too soon, they would realize Jon couldn't make street lights change with the wave of a hand and my genius ability was only a little common sense.

CHAPTER 14

Ready for School?

WE ARRIVED IN THE UNITED States in June, and Mary was enrolled in Kindergarten by September. It was amazing that she was fully capable of entering an all English speaking public school in just three months. She enjoyed school and was learning quickly while busily interacting with the other students. At the first parent/teacher conference, I chuckled at the teacher's stories of Mary at school and was pleased things were going well. As she told it, after a few days of class, Mary caught on to the order of things and decided the teacher could use some assistance. At the beginning of class, Mary would go up to the front of the room and stand by her teacher's desk. She would hand her whatever was next in the routine, already having the order memorized. When it was time for roll call, Mary would be standing in position, all ready with roll book in hand. She would hand the teacher the pen when it was time to mark in the book. Then she would hand her the chalk. After a time, some of the other students began protesting. They asked why Mary always got to do this daily task, to which the teacher answered, "Because Mary has initiative." She was an excellent teacher and from the beginning, she saw Mary's strengths and nurtured them with unusual insight.

Mary was quite excited to show me her schoolwork upon returning home each day. Toward the end of the first week of school, she pulled out a drawing from her backpack. She had used many bright colors, especially red, and she handed it to me with a big smile. "Teacher say draw what did at summertime," she said in her broken English. I reflected back on our trips to the beaches, the barbeques, visiting with grandparents and family and friends, and I smiled as I reached for the picture. But she had not drawn any of those activities. Apparently, in Romania, shortly before we left, the family had slaughtered a pig. This was all very standard there and a big deal as they would roast it whole with an added bonus of grilling the ears and tail to remove hair and make the outside crispy yet still chewy on the inside. This was a big treat for the children, and she reenacted the chewing when relaying the story to me. The drawing was well done, so there was no mistaking the carnage or the pig lying on its back with a knife stuck in it and blood everywhere, and the man (the stabber) standing over it. I was thankful for my lengthy chat with Mary's teacher about her history before the first day of school. Because of that chat, I didn't anticipate—neither did I receive—any alarmed calls from a school official or social worker requiring an explanation.

Michael was enrolled in preschool for three hours a day, and he loved it. One of his favorite things to do at home was to have one of us read from a set of children's Bible story encyclopedias. There were lots of full-sized colorful illustrations accompanying each story, and he was captivated. He even named his parakeet Noah. So it didn't surprise me when his teacher told me she thought Michael would be a pastor when he grew up as he loved talking about the Bible stories at school. Michael was at that preschool for two years until it was time for kindergarten. Those two years were crazy as I shuttled the three kids to and from school and other events. It was a busy time for me, as I also did the books and helped in other ways in our business, hosting and attending play dates and parties, and driving to Jon's many practices and games. Jon, now enrolled as a junior in high school, played baseball and soccer and also had taken piano lessons.

CHAPTER 15

Can Gheorghe find us?

WE DID HAVE SOME ONE-ON-ONE talks as Michael began to learn more English, and one of them was about Gheorghe. One day I was driving Michael home from preschool. He looked especially cute in his car seat with his rosy, chubby cheeks and striped polo shirt. He informed me that he knew what he was going to do when he grew up. I was happy about the topic Michael was bringing up, and my mind raced all over thinking of a policeman, or a fire fighter, a teacher, or maybe he would say working in construction like Brian. "What, Michael? What would you like to do when you grow up?" Michael answered very matter-of-factly that, when he grew up, he would go back to Romania and kill Gheorghe. Well, now, a quick glance back in my rearview mirror was still the image of a four-year-old angelic-looking child, and the words did not match. The wounds from Gheorghe were still fresh and raw. We talked about Gheorghe and why he was angry. I assured Michael that it was not his fault or the fault of the others around him whom Gheorghe treated so poorly. I tried to explain that Gheorghe made the wrong choice to take out his anger and frustration on others. In as simple terms as I could, I tried to describe a little of the hardship of life and the difficulty in making a living in Romania, the lack of conveniences and food, the horrible government.

Things were going well by day, but at night problems were surfacing. Michael had night terrors after falling asleep and was terrified Gheorghe would re-enter our lives. As much as we tried to comfort him, nothing was helping. He was not the least bit convinced we could not be outmaneuvered by the man who once held such control over him, his sister, and his mother. I spent a lot of bedtimes explaining that Gheorghe had no money to travel, but Michael's response was, "But what if he got some?" "Well, then the Romanian government would not let him leave." "But what if they did let him?" "Then our country would not let him enter. Our government is very strict on who can enter." "But what if they did let him come in?" "America is a very large country, and he does not know where we live. He could never find us." "But what if he did?" "Well, if he did, Daddy and Mommy would never let him get you." "What if you didn't see him or weren't home or I was outside?" Finally, we hit a homerun. "How about if we pray and ask Jesus to keep him away?" To my surprise, he looked relieved and agreed that this was the perfect and logical solution. I would begin the prayer and simply ask God to please not allow Gheorghe to come here. Michael would then pray the same thing. This continued every night for a few years and could never be skipped. We would pray other things as well during our bedtime prayers, but this was at the top of the list for a long time. So it came as a surprise when I once again began that part of the prayer and Michael politely let me finish and quietly said, "Mom, Gheorghe cannot get here. He doesn't have enough money, and if he did Romania would not let him leave. And if they did, America would not let him in. And if they did, he could never find us." So that was the end of Gheorghe's shadowy figure from the past lingering about. At last, it seemed, Michael was free.

When Michael was about six he began a conversation with me by saying that, when he was grown up, he would go back to Romania. He would go back, he said, to buy a truck and some tools for Gheorghe so he wouldn't be so angry, and he could build things and make more money, be happy, and be nice to people. I was glad to hear that he felt empowered and unaffected by Gheorghe and now desired to make a difference with goodness rather than violence.

One ordinary summer afternoon the doorbell rang, and Michael ran to the door and then called my name. Upon reaching the door, I found myself standing face to face with a salesperson who sported a determined expression. He immediately began his hard-sell spiel. I saw I could be trapped here for quite some time unless I put an immediate stop to it or bought something I didn't want. I said, "Sorry, but I have no money to buy anything." The salesperson didn't want to hang out any longer with the lady who had no money, and the door was shut in record time. It was then I heard loud sobbing from Michael's bedroom. I rushed to his room to assess the situation. He could barely speak through the sobs. Apparently, my words, "I have no money," had triggered this meltdown. He believed it was time that he would have to move along again to a new family who did have money. I explained as quickly as I could that we did have money in the bank; I just didn't have any in my purse at the moment. I explained that we had jobs and that Daddy was working. Then I clarified that, even if we didn't have money, we would still stick together no matter what. It took me a few times of repeating it all before he registered a look that convinced me he finally believed it to be true. Off he went to play with the kids in the cul-de-sac.

The kids had not been in school long when they began after school activities. Mary joined a jump rope class after school in the gym during second grade. After a short time she was invited to be part of a jump rope team. It was a delight to see that the bond between the eight girls in Mary's age group deepened while participating in competitions, performances, and travel as well as in life events. They became each other's advocates by loving and supporting each other throughout the elementary years and during the emotional changes and ups and downs coming on during the junior high and high school years. It was a busy and fun time.

Jon did well in high school and won a scholar/athlete award in his senior year. After graduating from high school he began attending the University of Washington majoring in business administration while working part time with Brian. During his college years he was still living at home and he was still very involved with the kids and continued to help them with homework when he wasn't busy with his own. After graduation he did some travelling then purchased a condo nearby our home.

Michael was in kindergarten when he started soccer after school. It was obvious Michael was smart as he could talk circles around us even as a young child and usually proved our points wrong by asking us a series of questions which lead to us contradicting ourselves by the end. Then he would simply say "got ya," and that would be the end of it because he had. He won some prizes for his drawings in elementary school and received the most inspirational award in high school tennis. He also participated in soccer, football, and wrestling during his growing up years, but by high school trouble was beginning to bubble under the surface.

In February 2006, just months before Michael was to graduate from high school, my mom was diagnosed with acute myeloid leukemia. The spring was difficult. She was in the hospital for over two and a half months, and she had to make many trips back to the clinic once she returned home. The summer was beautiful, and she was feeling better. Once again, life seemed normal as we took trips to the coast with Mom, Dad, and the family, and we shared root beer floats on their deck at home. Soon Christmas came, and Mom was once again admitted to the hospital. On a sunny spring day in March 2007, when the flowers were blooming and the sun was shining in its brilliance, Mom went very peacefully to heaven at about noon. Later that day, I drove Dad home. As we walked up the back steps, he gasped as he looked toward the backyard to see Mom's magnolia tree in full bloom. When I had picked up Dad in the morning, the blossoms had still been buds. I truly believe Mom saw her tree on the way to heaven. Somehow, it seemed, the perfectly radiant and golden spring day with blue sky, flowers, budding trees, and now the magnificence of the blooming magnolia tree had been orchestrated for her as she was ushered to heaven and bid the earth goodbye. She was an energetic and fun mom who left us with lots of life lessons and wonderful memories.

After Michael graduated from high school, toward the end of summer, we noticed a swelling on his neck. We took him to see his doctor, who took a blood draw for evaluation and speculated it could be mononucleosis. Test results came back negative, and so the doctor encouraged him in lifestyle changes such as more sleep and a better diet to build up his immune system. His neck was stiff and sore, so he also went to a chiropractor who thought the problem was his spine being out of alignment from sports. He believed that, after a few adjustments, Michael would feel better. Because of some uncharacteristic behavior consisting of anger and outbursts, Brian took Michael out for lunch, concerned now about the possibility of substance abuse. Brian confronted him and pressed him for answers. Finally Michael broke down and admitted addiction. He said it had begun with his prescription pain medication after an automobile accident two years earlier. Brian insisted he be admitted into a local rehab facility, Michael agreed, and we began making arrangements. We felt this could very well be the cause of his health problems.

During this time, when things were rocky, I decided to call a prayer line I had relied on many times before. I wanted prayer for the guys in my family—Brian, Jon, and Michael—as there were many issues they were dealing with. Michael was struggling with his latest drug-related difficulties, Jon was making decisions on basic life direction, and Brian had spent the last few years away from his faith and was showing little or no interest in the things of God. I had called this particular prayer line on other occasions for a variety of reasons, and after prayer, I had always felt hopeful again. Usually, I would speak with a kind woman who would ask my name, where I lived, a few basic questions, and lastly inquire of my prayer request. She would then pray skillfully, combining a heartfelt petition to God, woven with promises from scripture and statements of confident assurance that He was indeed listening and would work on our behalf, especially with our agreement in prayer together (Matthew 18:19).

This time it was not business as usual, however. The person who answered the phone that afternoon was an older man, and after he asked the regular questions, he asked me what I would like to pray about. After I detailed briefly my concerns, he was ready to go. He began praying for Brian, but shortly into his prayer, he stopped midsentence and paused. This was different. He said the Lord was telling him something. I had called this prayer line many times, and also other lines, but never had this happened. He went on to say the Lord was speaking to him, telling him that something big was about to happen. This "big thing" would bring Brian back to God. He said it would be like Paul's road-to-Damascus experience in the Bible (Acts 9:1–9), meaning the Lord would make Himself undeniably real in a powerful way, beyond what could be argued or reasoned away. He also said this event and the transformation in Brian would be key to changes in our family. He continued on to pray, powerfully and sweetly, for Jon, and then began his prayer for Michael. But he stopped midsentence once again. "The young one has a calling on his life," he said. By "a calling," I assumed he meant that God had a specific plan in ministry for him. It didn't surprise me, yet it did because of all our struggles. Something in me had known it from his days as a small child.

It was during the fall of 2007, only months after my mom went to heaven that Michael's headaches began, followed by doctors' appointments, chiropractic appointments, various antibiotics, and the time in rehab. When Michael's symptoms continued, finally a scan was ordered. I tried stifling the paralyzing feelings of fear and apprehension starting to rise up, and rather attempted to look toward God, whom I knew was a rock and a healer. Then, on January 23, 2008, a bomb dropped.

Adjusting to a new life back in the United States.

Two kids, a teenager, and a big fish.

Daddy and the kids.

The whole family.

US citizens!

The kids.

Some pretty good fishing.

Michael and his homework.

Story time with Daddy. All ages welcome.

Batman and Robin (a.k.a. Michael and our dog, Cappuccino).

Supergirl (a.k.a. Espresso, Michael's dog). She deserves a
spot here because she did turn out to be Supergirl, as she
was a great comforter to Michael during his difficult days.

The boys.

Sun River rafting with Jon and Mary.

Michael playing high school soccer.

PART
FIVE

Cancer

Though I walk through the valley
Of the shadow of death,
I will fear no evil;
For you are with me;
Your rod and your staff,
They comfort me.
You prepare a table before me
In the presence of my enemies.
—Psalm 23:4–5 (NKJV)

CHAPTER 16

A Frightening Diagnosis

JANUARY 23, 2008, WAS THE day the call came from the doctor's office. In the attempt to diagnose the cause of his headaches and fatigue, after all other efforts were exhausted, Michael had undergone a scan. It was discovered that there was a large tumor in his head. The nurse, who was making this most difficult call, was making it because the doctor was not in the clinic that day. I will never forget the grace and tenderness with which she relayed this most dreadful news. She explained the horrible facts of this tumor's existence and then, with barely a breath between her words, she threw me a lifeline of hope. She said it was likely Hodgkin's lymphoma, a type of cancer that is very treatable. Patients normally respond to treatment quickly, and the cure rate is high. Of course, we would not know the type of tumor for sure until an aspiration had been done and the results were returned from the lab. She had given us hope, and I was grateful.

The day we went for this procedure was dark and dreary weather-wise and in every other possible way. Michael was in pain as I sat with him waiting with all the other terrified patients and families in the biopsy waiting room. At last, his name was called, and I escorted him back with the nurse and stayed with him until the procedure began. My sister, Laurie, arrived and stayed with me in the waiting room.

Finally, he was finished. A large bandage had been placed on his neck where the incision had been made.

Agonizing days went by as Michael's pain intensified and we faced the fact that we were not dealing with a problem a stronger antibiotic, a series of chiropractic appointments, or a month in rehab could remedy. And so began the tidal wave of appointments around which life would revolve for an uncertain amount of time. We would need to get Michael's hearing, heart, and teeth checked and begin our appointments with his primary oncologist and the radiation oncologist. It was about this time we received news that the results of Michael's aspiration procedure were inconclusive as to the type of cancer we were dealing with. We needed to return to have a larger biopsy.

We met with Michael's oncologist and later the radiation oncologist. I was impressed with the knowledge and professionalism both of them displayed. We felt we were in the best of hands. When we met with the radiation oncologist, he sat alongside a white board displaying a list of possible cancers it could be. He had a new one on the list. It was nasopharyngeal carcinoma. He mentioned that the nasopharyngeal tumor type had the potential to shrink the fastest and hoped this was what we were dealing with. He explained the maximum number of radiation treatments that could be given is thirty-five. These must be administered consecutively for five days, Monday through Friday. Saturday and Sunday would be rest days. This would continue for seven weeks with no breaks. He explained it would be challenging to make it through this treatment to the end, but it was critical to do so. Each day of the prescribed treatment skipped or postponed could lower the success rate significantly. This regimen would also be difficult because of the strength of the chemotherapy that needed to be done in congruence with the radiation treatments. This tumor must shrink and die in the time allotted.

All this information was well presented, and I was taking notes so I could remember and explain it correctly to others. We finally got news of the latest biopsy result. The diagnosis was nasopharyngeal carcinoma. This was the best-case scenario, we had been told, because of its ability to shrink quickly.

We wanted the treatment to begin and have it all over and in our past as quickly as possible. Of course, we had to do everything in a certain order. There was much preparation to be done, and so we occupied our time with the many tasks ahead. Radiation can damage the teeth, so we made a dental appointment for deep cleaning. A heart examination was ordered to evaluate the strength of his heart for such challenging treatment ahead. The EKG showed stress to his heart. Ear and throat exams were necessary. The ear examination revealed that Michael's hearing had become severely impaired on one side because the tumor pressing on the area. All this was extremely difficult, and every day seemed so dark and dreary. I struggled to keep my mind on God and His promises, knowing this was my only hope in coping with the devastation we were dealing with.

Of course, I understood that sometimes God calls people home to heaven sooner than we want, for His purposes and for reasons we will know only after we get to heaven. But I didn't believe this was God's will for Michael. I believed that God had big plans on earth for Michael, that cancer was the enemy, and He would see us through somehow. I had read several books and testimonies over the years about God healing people, including a short book by Dodie Osteen called *Healed of Cancer*. I believed from all I had read that I should not focus on how negative the report or how dire the symptoms appeared. These were circumstances, and circumstances could change. After all, consider Dodie Osteen's story. We had been given hope, she had been given none, yet she continued to fight on believing day after day that God could and would heal her according to the promises in the Bible. Inspired by her testimony and many other similar testimonies, I made the decision to stand in faith as well. It was still not easy, and a fierce battle for my emotions was on. This was another pivotal moment as I decided even more firmly that I would attempt to direct my thoughts toward the promises in the Bible for Michael's complete healing rather than dwell on an alternate outcome.

The doctors gave us the best-case scenarios but were frank about the other possibilities. A PET scan was ordered, which would show all the cancer in Michael's body. It was an uncomfortable and long process because he would need to lie still in various positions for periods of time that could be unbearable because of the pain he was experiencing. The oncologist told us the results would come back in a few days, and he would call us personally with the results. This was of particular concern because both oncologists informed us about all that hinged on this very important scan. This report would tell us all we needed to know—all that could be known according to current medical standards. If the cancer was contained in the head and neck area, it was treatable and likely curable provided Michael's tumor shrank during the time allotted for radiation and chemo treatment. If the cancer was not contained in the head and neck area but had shown up anywhere below that area of his body, there would still be treatment to prolong life, but there would be no medical cure.

One miserable day, Michael and I sat at the conference table across from our radiation oncologist in his office. The doctor looked directly into our eyes with a look of deep concern. "I am worried," he remarked as both Michael and I sat in stunned silence. I had counted on him to tell us we were in the best-case scenario category and that Michael's tumor would shrink quickly within the thirty-five-radiation-treatment time zone. Why wasn't he saying this now? Why was he worried? I didn't want to know, but of course we had to know. These were honest as well as compassionate doctors, so they would disclose the whole story, not just the part that was most comfortable to discuss. He was deeply concerned about the upcoming PET scan results. Apparently, the tumor had grown so large there was a high risk that cancer cells could have traveled elsewhere in the body. If that were the case, he continued, we could only buy Michael some time, maybe at the most three years, in the hopes a cure could be found. I clung to the hope, with all the resolve I had, that the PET scan would give us a good report. I did not believe there would be a cure discovered within three years, and I sensed by the expression on his face that the doctor didn't either.

We left the hospital that afternoon and were driving home when I said to Michael the only thing I could think of that was significant, which was, "Let's pray." And so we did. I prayed for Michael. I prayed that the scan would show positive results. I prayed that we would get through this and past this, and that God would touch him and heal him. I prayed all would be well and that Michael would have a bright future beyond all we were facing. I had not heard Michael pray for years—not many times anyway, since he had been a little guy when I listened to his bedtime prayers. I reflected back to the days when Michael asked Jesus to not let Gheorghe come to America. I had no idea at this point where he was with his faith as he had declined to speak of it for a few years. However, out of his mouth came the most beautiful and bravest of prayers. He asked God that the scan would be positive. He prayed for God to heal him and help him get through the treatments. And then he prayed, "But, God, if it is not to be, then I will come joyfully to you with open arms." I was stunned and heartbroken that a young person, only a few months after his twentieth birthday, would even need to pray such a thing. It was a difficult prayer for me to hear because, in my thoughts and heart, I so didn't want to go there, yet it gave me comfort to know he was turning to God in this great time of need.

We did not receive a call about the PET scan after several days, so I called as the weekend was upon us and I assumed there would be no call during that time. The report had still not been sent to the doctor, and so our fate and future would be unknown throughout the weekend. This, it seemed, would be a long, painful, anxious wait. But then on Sunday morning, when I imagined no cancer clinic is open anywhere, Michael's oncologist called. He had checked his computer that morning to find that Michael's report had come through late the day before. He quickly gave us the news that the cancer had not traveled beyond the head and neck area. I felt a barrage of emotion including joy, relief, and thankfulness. I was so grateful that our doctor chose to call on a Sunday to share good news. Brian and I sat on our stairs with tears of gratitude on our faces.

This news was a relief, but there was still much work to be done. Michael needed to have a port-a-cath surgically inserted. The catheter, which is a tube that connects to a port placed under the skin in a vein near the shoulder, is used for blood draws and the administration of medications such as chemo and hydrating solutions. This would mean he wouldn't have to be stuck with needles or have intravenous therapy (IVs) numerous times a week. This was a surgery that took place in the hospital. Then there was even a more difficult surgery to insert a feeding tube through the wall of his stomach. After the surgeries, he had one tube hanging out of his chest and one hanging out of his stomach. The reason for the feeding tube was that the radiation treatment would cause burns on his mouth, throat, and tongue. According to the radiation oncologist, these areas become so burned it is nearly impossible to swallow liquid and even more difficult to eat food. He described it as the sensation of having shards of glass stuck down the entire throat. He explained there would be a period of time also when Michael would be unable to speak. He also mentioned that a few patients had refused the feeding tube, feeling they would manage okay. Some of those people became dangerously malnourished, which threatened the success of their treatment. We opted to have the feeding tube installed with this persuasive information at hand. The surgery for the feeding tube was difficult and more painful to recover from than the port-a-cath surgery, but we turned the corner on that.

The next step was to have a radiation mask made by the techs in the radiation department. Meanwhile, there was much preparation going on behind the scenes. MRIs had been done to measure the exact size, shape, and location of the tumor. This information was digitalized and loaded into a computer that would process the information, map it out, and on its own develop a precise target area, skillfully dodging and avoiding all healthy, valuable tissue and nearby glands from the harmful rays intended to annihilate the tumor. At one point, when the beginning treatment date was moved out, the reasoning, we were told, was that the computer had not yet finished "thinking" and had not yet revealed the plan. As anxious as we were to get the show on the road, we certainly didn't want to interfere with the computer or anyone else involved in formulating the perfect plan. It was a state-of-the art system, we were told, and many hospitals did not own such sophisticated equipment. Without this equipment, in some patients, glands that were near the areas that were to be radiated, most notably the saliva glands, suffered irreparable damage.

It was a heartbreaking task to awaken Michael every day and get him to the car. When we got to the hospital, I would drop him off at the front door, and he would either make it down the escalator to the cancer clinic or wait on a bench while I parked and retrieved a wheelchair. If he made it himself, I would hurry as fast as possible to the waiting room of the cancer clinic only to find Michael lying on a couch obviously in very bad shape. The other waiting patients looked alarmed as they glanced his direction, and we were always very quickly ushered into an area in the back for bloodwork and then to an exam room where he could lie down. We were fortunate in that every single one of these professionals—from the receptionists, to the aids, nurses, and doctors—were always kind and helpful.

Lonnie was the mom of one of Michael's friends. She sent me an email one day asking if she could come and help. The logistics of getting Michael from the car to a wheelchair and then downstairs to the cancer clinic were tricky because I had to leave him alone while I parked the car. When she offered to be at the unloading zone with a wheelchair, I was more than happy to take her up on it. I'll never forget the day I drove into the hospital loading zone to see Lonnie standing there, grasping the handles of a wheelchair, ready for action. From that day forward, she was there daily, giving whatever support she could in her unassuming and sensitive way. My sisters, Nancy, Laurie, and Jane were also there to assist in any way they could, logging in many hours at the hospital. My dad came when he could. Brian's sister, Barbara, lived out of state but called often and sent gifts to help keep Michael occupied during treatment. And Brian's brother, Doug, was always offering help. Brian's sister, Diane, and her husband, Larry, brought dinners every Thursday night. What a treat to find those delicious meals waiting in the refrigerator when we got home after a long and exhausting day. The pastors from Washington Cathedral, Tim and Jackie White prayed for Michael daily. Tim, along with his father Pastor Dale White came to our home several times, anointed Michael with oil and prayed for him. Pastor Michael Fernandez also visited Michael in the hospital many times. We consider them lifelong friends and are grateful for their love and care over the years.

The day the radiation mask was made is a bit of a blur. In the radiation oncology department, Michael lay on the table where the radiation was actually to be given, and at this point more calculations were made. Michael was ushered into an interior room lined with glass windows on one side. It might be a fascinating process to watch, but not when it is your son. I stood in disbelief with many emotions—thankfulness for the help and advanced treatment we were receiving, shock that all this was happening, and numbness of some sort that I assumed was God's protective shield to keep me from completely crumbling. I didn't always feel God's presence, especially during these times, but I knew He was with us because, in the Bible, He said He would be (Hebrews 13:5b). When I was home, I would go into the office, shut the door, lie on the couch, and turn on instrumental Christian music. Then I could sense His presence. I was bathed in His love and strength and the peace that the Bible says "surpasses all understanding" (Philippians 4:7). And, for sure, it did. It was during those moments as I lay relaxing in His love and company that anxiety and turmoil quieted down.

We also met with the pharmacists to go over the chemotherapy drugs and other accompanying medications. Here we were presented with pages of side effects with nightmarish potential consequences. There we would sit while the information was recited thoroughly, and Michael had to initial each item and sign at the bottom. I wanted to protect him from this information, but of course, he was of age. All of it was directed toward him, and it was his signature that was required. But, on a daily basis, I was finding that my youngest was courageous, and I was proud and amazed at him time and time again.

CHAPTER 17

Care Pages.com

I HAD THE UNPLEASANT JOB of notifying family and friends about everything that was happening, and I was thankful for email so that I didn't have to make individual phone calls, which would have been quite time consuming and emotionally draining. My sister, Jane, told me about CarePages.com and sent me a link to sign up. This was very helpful. Through this site we could keep friends and family members informed, and they could sign up to be notified of updates. It could all be done in one tidy package, letting everyone know at once about the most recent events. There was also a place for the online visitors to leave messages if any wished to do so. This was not to replace conversation, I explained in an initial email; it was only meant to help me provide a speedier account of recent happenings. Anyone was welcome to call anytime.

The following CarePages updates are excerpts from some of the chronicled entries of a few of the days we faced. To the many who prayed, as well as to those who made dinners, brought gifts, communicated well wishes, sent flowers, cards, and balloons we will always be grateful. There also were many responses to these and the other CarePages entries full of friendship, love, and encouragement, all of which made a tremendous difference for us during these days.

Posted February 8, 2008—11:07 p.m.

All of you who are visiting this care page for Michael have probably heard by now that he was diagnosed recently with a rare cancer (rare in the US) called nasopharyngeal. It apparently started in the airspace behind the nose and above the roof of the mouth called the nasopharynx. He had a PET scan last week. As the doctors explained it to us, the results would determine if it was curable or not curable. If it had not spread, it could be treated and most likely cured. If it had spread, there would be no cure, and they could only buy us some time in the hopes a cure could be found. We did get the results of the PET scan, and it came back with no evidence of having spread beyond the head and neck area (*very good!*). The treatment is harsh but should be very effective.

Michael has been amazingly brave through all of this, and I have been proud of him. The doctors don't hold back any information, but he has handled it with grace and faith. I have seen no sign of the little boy who used to make the doctors or nurses chase him around the examination table, especially if there was a needle involved.

I will keep everyone updated as much as possible. Until then, we thank you so much for your prayers.

Posted February 14, 2008—10:11 p.m.

Today was hard, but we are finally on our way. Treatment began this morning with radiation. That was a very emotional moment for me, but Michael was amazing. He just doesn't complain. He had previously had a radiation mask molded to his face which was put on and snapped into place. The mask is marked

94

with the spots to target. Of course, the targeting is much more sophisticated than that, with computerized images showing a lot of intricate detail. After he was put on the table and the mask snapped into place, I was taken to an area where I could see it all on computer screens. It is amazing to watch, and only took a short time—between fifteen and twenty minutes.

Then we went to the cancer center where they gave him an infusion to hydrate and prevent nausea. This took two hours. The chemo drip came next, which took one hour. So the treatment has begun, and tomorrow is more of the same. Thanks for caring and checking in. Happy Valentine's Day, and I will report in again tomorrow night.

Posted February 25, 2008—11:23 p.m.

"Early and remarkable" were the words Michael's radiation oncologist used today to describe the tumor's response to its double attack from the chemo and radiation. Later this week the plan is to do a new CT scan so they can adjust the radiation to the smaller-sized tumor. This was especially positive news after hearing the doctor tell us that, if the tumor hadn't begun to shrink by this point, he would be directing us toward hospice planning. He mentioned that the tumor had been a stage 4A carcinoma and already had begun eating the bone at the base of the skull. He said that this shrinkage was a major milestone and congratulated us all. Michael's regular oncologist had also remarked that the tumor was receding more quickly than anticipated. It's clear to me that prayers are being answered.

Thanks for checking in.

Posted March 9, 2008—9:13 p.m.

Friday night, after a day of chemo and radiation, Michael was busy. He had dinner with a friend, went to a late movie, and then came home in a very talkative mood. Brian and I were asleep and quite tired, so I can't remember a word of the conversation. Basically, all I remember is a noisy shadow by the side of the bed, but he was having fun and enjoying life, and that's the only message that got through to me.

On Saturday, Michael was exhausted from the chemo catching up to him, so he stayed in bed the whole day, which was fine since he has his own personal servants. I am getting in shape running up and down the stairs fetching and retrieving, Mary was doing his laundry and cleaning his room. Brian ran to Taco Time for him in the morning.

Sunday has now come, and Michael is emerging from his room at about 3:00 p.m. This is happening because Brian, Jon, and he are going to the mall to get Michael a new computer. All of his relatives on both sides of the family—aunts, uncles, grandmas, grandpas, cousins, (and us)—have all put money together to buy Michael a new laptop computer to help occupy him during the recovery process. The family has been very generous, so the guys are off to buy Michael his choice of computer.

Tomorrow begins a new week, and we are counting on no nausea. The further away from chemo we get, the happier we will be. Michael has another new mouth wash/ gargle/ rinse to add to his repertoire. We have a prescription strength aloe vera mixture for coating and healing his mouth and throat; a homemade salt, water, and baking soda mixture for taking away the unsavory tastes that chemo leaves;

and a lidocaine liquid to coat and numb the mouth and throat. Lately we have acquired a powder to be mixed into gel form immediately before use, with one tablespoon of water. This also coats the mouth and throat with even stronger and longer-lasting numbing qualities. This one is to be used at night directly before bed and is to help the comfort level for falling asleep. Its effectiveness should last throughout the night and into the morning so that there is also more comfort upon waking. This list does not include the tablets, capsules, creams, and patches we have in our medicine bag. That's okay ... we are very happy to have them! They are working nicely to take the edge off and to make those side effects relatively tolerable.

God has been very faithful to us through this whole ordeal, and the evidence of answered prayer is something we see every day. Thank you, everyone, for checking up on Michael and for all of your love and prayers which have helped so much and have meant so much to us during this time!

Posted March 26, 2008—11:06 p.m.

Thirty radiation treatments done, and five more to go! Michael's mouth is officially *sore*. The skin on one side of his tongue is burned, and that does not make life easy or fun, but true to form, Michael is not complaining. I can tell it hurts because his eyebrows go up in the middle. Like this: / \. Not quite as dramatic as my illustration, but that's what they did when he was a little guy and unhappy, and that's what they are doing now at times. He is making a valiant effort toward normalcy, trying to eat even though everything mouth-related hurts, and food tastes strange. Last night he went out to eat and bowl. The night before that he was out, and the night before that was bowling also. He is slowing down a bit, but for such times, he has his computer (thanks, relatives!), which has been a great source of entertainment and distraction for him. It accompanies him to the hospital every day, and he is busy doing all kinds of fun things on it.

The next few weeks will be a challenge—getting through the last main chemo, the last five radiations, and then a few weeks that follow. Apparently, these weeks can be difficult because the radiation keeps building up even after the treatments have been completed. The chemo oncologist said that many people are hospitalized during these subsequent weeks for pain management.

Thank you, family members and friends, for being there and for all the many ways you show that you care. You all have helped us tremendously as we have faced this challenge. God has been our rock every step of the way and has answered so many of our prayers.

Posted April 3, 2008—12:40 a.m.

The long-awaited last day of radiation finally happened, and what a day! The sun was shining radiantly, and the flowers all seemed to be blooming for our good fortune. We began the day in the cancer center with hydration, pain medication, anti-nausea medicine, and the last of the Amifostine, a drug to protect the saliva glands. Michael presented the front desk cancer clinic people with a box of See's chocolates for all of their thoughtfulness. He had another box for the nurse's station in the back. He was all hooked up to his IV pole, pulling it along as he went, delivering the gifts. We had a fruit bouquet sent to the radiation team (since they always seem to be dieting—no candy for them). There was joy in the air, and we got many congratulations, and Michael received a certificate of completion from the radiation staff signed by them all, including the doctor. His radiation mask is officially retired from service and is now just a souvenir.

Thank you all for checking up on Michael.

Posted April 8, 2008—10:40 a.m.

Michael's radiation treatment is over, but as predicted, the effects are pretty harsh. Michael is very brave and stoic, but the radiation has burned his neck, the inside of his throat, and his tongue. As the doctors had indicated, the burns have become worse after the treatment has stopped because of the cumulative effects of radiation. He is on his pain medicine and is hanging in there, still going to the clinic every day. The nurse yesterday had a chuckle when she heard that Michael had spent some time at the mall, at a friend's house, and even went bowling again over the weekend. The rest of the time he kicked back at home and rested.

Since his throat hurts, he is speaking very little, and because he can't swallow, his nourishment is coming from the feeding tube. He has become very creative with sign language and notes, thumbs up or down, and lots of text messaging. I was at the clinic last week with Michael when I got a text message. It was from Michael, who was right there. I'm a very slow text messenger, and had it on the wrong mode, and was trying to write a reply when I looked up at Michael who was looking at me as if I had lost my mind. Then it suddenly dawned on me—I could talk!!

They say it will be about a week, and then he will turn the corner and start healing from the side effects of treatment. Thanks for all of your prayers. At this point it's a little rough, but pretty soon I will be reporting that life for Michael is returning to normal.

End of CarePages.

These CarePages entries represent an upbeat version of those days, but there was much more going on behind the scenes. It was like a roller coaster on a fast track that could shoot any direction without warning and leave any one of us deposited a mile down a new road in a blink of the eye. There were also times when I was simply too tired to sort it all out and write it down.

People were continually asking me how I was holding up. It was an extremely difficult time, obviously, and there were many shattering moments, but there were things I relied on to help me cope. Years earlier and long before the news Michael had cancer, I had developed the habit of a daily quiet time with God. It was a relatively small amount of time that consisted of some Bible reading and reciting a list of declarations or positive confessions based on scriptural promises from the Bible, which were on a typed and now-tattered few sheets of paper. These confessions/promises were personalized, and I would read them aloud, the idea being that we are created in the image of God, and He creates by speaking and so do we by our negative words or our positive words.

The power behind these positive-word confessions was enhanced because of the bedrock of truth coming from God's own promises to us based on scripture. Also, this activity is rooted in the principle that we believe the very words we speak ourselves. It can work negatively as well; for instance, when we tell the same lie over and over, we begin, unintentionally, blurring the truth from even ourselves and eventually can be given over to believing the very lie meant only to deceive others. But as we speak the personalized promises from God, we begin to believe them ourselves, and so our faith grows. In this daily quiet time, as I mentioned before, I would also spend a few minutes "soaking" or relaxing in the presence of God. I would turn on instrumental worship music and just get quiet. It was during these times that He would give me answers to questions or a verse that would help in a pertinent, timely manner. Sometimes I simply gained strength, encouragement, direction, hope, or simply joy from being with Him during that time. Life's challenges can bring wounds that go deep into the soul, and it was during these quiet times with God that I felt my soul being restored. This daily time with God was my lifeline.

It was hard to say how Brian was coping. In his profession, it is his job to build or repair things, so when the kids were little, they could bring just about anything to Brian and he could fix it. If a bike or a toy was broken he would either repair it or buy a new one. He was also their protector and made them feel safe. So when Michael developed stage-four cancer, Brian was utterly helpless to change the direction. All he could do was try to focus on his work and pay the bills, but it was devastating to him feeling powerless to help when his young son needed him the most.

During the time after Michael's diagnosis but shortly before treatment, Brian and I thought I should call Rodica and ask her to alert the children's birth mother, Lenuta, in Romania. I had maintained contact with her over the years, sending letters, but more often only padded envelopes with stacks of pictures. It was a chore to get letters translated, and I more often than not got the job done by stuffing an envelope with a pile of recent photos. The pictures were always darling since the kids were continually active, so Lenuta received smiling happy faces with the children participating in a variety of parties, school events, sports, vacations, picnics, and other fun activities. It seemed to me these told the story better than words could express anyway. How was I going to tell Lenuta about Michael's condition after sending all of those smiling pictures?

Since Rodica's family still resided in the same village as Lenuta, we felt it would be best for them to relay the information concerning Michael to Lenuta instead of us telling her in a letter. There was also the option of doing nothing at all, even though I couldn't conceive of keeping this secret from her. Rodica agreed to have her mother, in Somesu Rece, contact Lenuta with the recent findings regarding Michael, accompanied with the explanation that, according to the doctors, he would most likely be cured after treatment was completed. I did, however, receive a call from Rodica a day or so later with a proposal for an alternate plan. Rodica's family in Romania felt it would be best to wait and tell Lenuta only after Michael had recovered from treatment and the danger had been passed. Their reasoning was that, when a diagnosis such as Michael's is given in Romania, it is a certain death sentence because of the lack of updated equipment. Rodica's family wanted Lenuta to be spared the worry and be notified once the treatment was completed and Michael's status was safely in the cured zone. I was agreeable to this plan, trusting Rodica and her family to have an understanding of the culture and the best way of handling this in the most sensitive manner.

Rodica was not done unveiling her alternative plan, however, and the next phase—part two—was quite interesting. She and Cornell had come up with the idea to fly Lenuta to Seattle. She would arrive once treatment had ended and Michael had recovered sufficiently. Since communication with Lenuta had to be in the Romanian language, she would stay with them and then reconnect with the children at some point and see for herself that Michael was well. This was a perfect plan, and I was thrilled with the possibility. I had always wanted to connect the children with Lenuta again, feeling that my job in this area would be done and they could, from there, form whatever bond they were all comfortable with. This would be a great opportunity to put closure on the past while opening a door for the future. I loved the new and improved plan which, hopefully, would be shaping up soon.

Michael's high school senior picture.

Michael and Lisa, high school graduation, 2006.

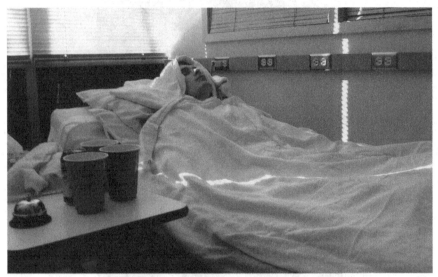
Diagnosed with cancer, January 2008.

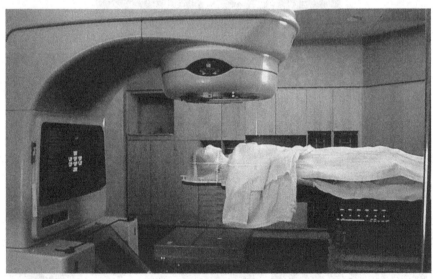
Radiation treatment begins.

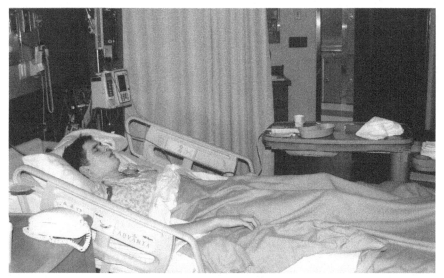

Chemotherapy begins.

Elena, Rodica, Lenuta, Mary, Michael,
Cornell, Brian and Lisa, 2008.

PART
SIX

Stunning
Developments

Truth is stranger than fiction, but it is because fiction
is obliged to stick to possibilities; Truth isn't.
—Mark Twain

CHAPTER 18

Another Frightening Diagnosis

AFTER MICHAEL HAD COMPLETED THE radiation and chemotherapy, during which time the healing of his throat, mouth, and neck were in full swing, Lenuta arrived in Seattle. Life was scheduled to be better any day now when suddenly Michael began feeling worse. It made sense when the doctor mentioned the complexity of introducing solid food back into his system, which had grown accustomed to a liquid diet. It was normal for his digestive tract to protest a bit, so we were not overly concerned. Michael's appetite, after initially revving up, was now decreasing. He was eating less solid food and began losing weight, so we had no choice but to increase the feeding tube canned nutrition option again. I would ask Michael what he felt like eating in an effort to keep his solid food intake happening, and he would think about it and give me an answer. After a trip to the store and preparing his choice of food, we would watch him take a bite or two and set it down. He had no appetite and simply could not eat. He was in obvious discomfort. Progress seemed to have halted, and he was beginning a backward slide. His doctors ordered a CT scan. I did not expect a negative result, yet in the back of my mind there was a nagging feeling that I was attempting to ignore while trying to stay in faith that God's healing power was working in Michael's case.

The morning arrived when we were doing our routine of blood work at the cancer care clinic. The doctor entered the room with a solemn expression and the inconceivable announcement that Michael had a spot in his hip bone, according to the recently returned results of the CT scan. Now we were plunged into one of the darkest days of our journey. My mind was a blur as the statements from the doctor, at the beginning of all this, came spinning back hitting me with force and swirling around like a descending tornado. "There is no cure if cancer is found below the head and the neck area." "We can perhaps buy him three years in hopes a cure may be found." "I'm worried about the PET scan results." And now here we were. The doctor ordered a bone marrow biopsy to be done immediately. This was turning out to be one of the worst days of my entire life.

I took Michael into the diagnostic imaging waiting room and was feeling shocked and dazed over all these new events that were so quickly developing. It had been only about a year before this that I had been wheeling my very sick mother into this same waiting room, and I could almost see us there—we were right over there in those chairs the first time, and over that direction the second. And the last ... well, over in that corner. Before Michael's feeding tube was to be put in, he was lying on the bench over there. And now, when he was supposed to be better, we were back here once again, and I felt an almost overwhelming battle in my mind and emotions. Finally, we were called in and directed to a room. The surgeon arrived, accompanied by a nurse who brought her smile and calming manner into the room. She radiated comfort, and for some reason I felt a little better. The surgeon chatted with me about treatment options for tumor elimination and mentioned that, as soon as he retrieved the bone marrow specimen from Michael's hip bone, he would know by sight if it was cancer. Michael's oncologist stopped by and encouraged me not to jump to conclusions but to just wait and see.

I sat alone but was fine with it because I could talk to God. He would help me feel better and give me hope. He always did, and the nurse's kindness and competent manner helped too. I was allowed to stay during the procedure, and I watched as the doctor began the biopsy. It was a fairly quick but unpleasant process, and I was watching intently the faces of both the doctor and the nurse to see their reaction as they pulled the specimen out and placed it in the container for the lab. The doctor had already disclosed that they would immediately know if it was cancer or not, but their faces remained expressionless as they were dealing with the sample. I asked the doctor if it was cancer, and he would not answer my question. "The sample must go to pathology, and your oncologist will receive the report and notify you of the results." That was all he would say.

The doctor and the nurse left the room while Michael groaned in pain, and I sat there attempting to bolster my faith, keeping my hope in God's healing power and promises. I decided to find the nurse. I found her in the hallway. I looked squarely into her eyes and asked point blank, "Is it cancer?" She kept my gaze, never flinching or looking away, and answered my question. "Yes" was all she said. I thanked her for telling me. I was very appreciative she had done so, sparing me the wait. I walked back into Michael's room. Michael was in a great deal of pain. He was receiving pain medicine through his port, but once pain was established, it was harder to reverse and relieve it. Laurie showed up, and it was nice having the support and the company. The oncologist came by and made the decision to admit Michael into the hospital for pain management. Brian, Jon, and Mary headed for the hospital as did my other sisters.

Once situated in the hospital room Michael continued having difficulty, but the nurses and aids were attending to him. His complexion had developed a gray tone, which Laurie detected first. At one point, while talking to Nancy, I noticed Laurie and Jane talking outside the door and so I stepped out to join them for a moment. It was several months later when I learned what Laurie and Jane's hallway conversation had been about, and I am glad I didn't know at the time. I began to cry when I joined them in the hallway, as the thought slammed into me that Michael could be getting ready to go to heaven. When I alluded to that idea, I noticed Laurie and Jane briefly exchange glances, and wondered if they were having similar thoughts. I couldn't even imagine it, and I knew the gaping hole in our family would be massive without Michael.

The confidential interaction between Laurie and Jane in the hallway, which I learned of later, was about a dream Laurie had on more than one occasion prior to the disastrous developments of the day. Mom was in the dream looking radiantly beautiful as if in heaven. Laurie, after greeting her, asked what she was doing, to which Mom calmly replied that she was "waiting." Puzzled, Laurie inquired as to what she was waiting for. Mom's calm and matter-of-fact response was simply, "Michael." When she shared this with Jane, she received a reaction she was not expecting. Jane had a very similar dream at least once and also decided it should be kept secret; that is, until the moment in the hallway talking with Laurie. They realized they both had one of their dreams of Mom waiting for Michael on the same night.

It was there in the hallway, not even knowing their conversation, that I could not avoid looking head on at the possibility that this story may have an unwanted outcome, which I had avoided entertaining at any cost in my attempt to walk in faith and be positive for Michael. I never wanted Michael to see anything on my face other than the complete assurance that we would get through this. Ultimately, Michael was in God's hands, I had to remind myself, and I could trust Him. At that moment, the possibility that I could recover from such sorrow seemed insurmountable, so I stepped back into the hospital room to see what needed to be done.

Later that night Mary sent out this CarePages entry:

Posted June 4, 2008—11:47 p.m.

Hey everyone! Michael and my mom are staying at the hospital tonight. Michael was admitted today because he wasn't feeling well. We could really use your prayers during this time, and always, as Michael is working to fight for his health. My mom will be posting an update as soon as she can, but she wanted me to write and ask for prayers. Thank you so much for your love and support. We love you all.

Mary

People left many messages on all of our CarePages entries. I have not included them because there were many, but I will add a few to these next entries to illustrate the kind of support and prayers we received from friends and family members. All of the messages throughout the duration of our CarePages entries as well as all messages from emails, phone calls, cards, and other communications brought much comfort to us, and the prayers were of immense value.

Mary W – June 5, 2008
Hang in there!

I've been wondering how you have been doing. Michael, I'm so sorry to hear you are at the hospital tonight. Given the lousy weather, it would not be a good night for a boat ride on the lake anyway! Mary

Julianne D – June 5, 2008
We are thinking of you!

Hey Mikey B!
Juan and I are thinking of you always. We love you so much and hope you start feeling better soon. Keep your good spirits strong. We know you will get through this period. We'll keep praying for you.

Love you!
Julianne and Juan

Misha M – June 5, 2008
Love

I love you, Michael. Stay strong. I'm praying and thinking of you.

Paula S – June 5, 2008
You've got it!

Praying and fighting the good fight for you with everything I've got!!!

Love, Paula

Laurie D – June 5, 2008
Love you Mikey B

We love you!

Mark & Emily T – June 5, 2008
Hope you're okay

We've heard the latest through Nancy. We're praying, and we hope the pain is retreating and that you can go home soon. We love you!

Jackie W – June 5, 2008
Prayers

Hi Mary,
Thanks for sending out the update for your mom. Michael is in all of our prayers. We spent time at our staff meeting today praying for him, and Tim and I are praying for him continually during this time. We have

hope and faith that God's going to bring him through this next challenge ... and prayers for the entire family.

Much love,
Jackie and Pastor Tim

Mary L – June 5, 2008

Michael,
Am fiercely praying for you to get better. God will work it all out.

Love, Mary

Katie P – June 5, 2008
Feel better!

Hi, Michael and Bate family. You are all in my thoughts and prayers during this time. Michael, I hope you begin feeling better very soon.

Katie P

Posted June 6, 2008-11:00pm by Lisa

It has been a wild last couple of days, and we are attempting to make sense of it all and come up with the perfect plan. We are studying up on all of our options because it was unfortunately discovered that there is some cancer in Michael's hip bone. This became a source of a good deal of pain, thereby contributing to the reason for his night in the hospital. The doctors and nurses proved to be masters at pain management, and even though it took a bit of time, they were able to do the job. We are considering several new treatment options, and with each option there is more chemotherapy. He will have a PET scan on Tuesday to determine if this is an isolated occurrence, which we are praying is the case, and also praying that it can be addressed and eliminated in a speedy fashion.

Now that the pain is better, Michael has once again resumed his usual zest for life. He visited friends right after he returned from the hospital yesterday and is right now at another friend's house. Michael is inspiring me with his courage in the face of this adversary and is handling it all with a great deal of composure. He participates in the conversations with the doctors asking questions, adding comments and corrections where he feels it necessary. During his hospital stays, he is very careful to regulate the nurses in their dispensing of his medications and in exactly how to do his blood draws. Even though he makes sure everyone is on task, he has been polite and courteous to those who are tending to him, saying please and thank you and in one instance getting a bit carried away with "I hope you are still here tomorrow ...pleaassssee ... what will I do without you?" all the while fake crying to a nurse with one of his silly smiles, making us all laugh.

Please continue to keep us all in your prayers. Thank you so much! ~Lisa

Dorothy Bate – June 7, 2008
Calling in the big guns

Dear Michael,
I called in a couple of groups of prayer warriors I know, average age about eighty-five, so they are seasoned prayers, experienced and tough.

That cancer doesn't stand a chance. Waves of love and healing are washing over you right now. God is with you all the way. Love, Grandma

Denise D – June 7, 2008
Love you!

More prayer is on the way!

Jacob C – June 7, 2008
Hey Michael

Mike,
I am sorry to hear of this recent update. I will definitely have my church praying for you this week. Bud (our old soccer coach) says hi, and we talk about you weekly. I am sorry I have not made it out to see you yet, but as such, things have been a little crazy. Please know that you are in my thoughts and prayers. If you would like someone just to talk to email me.

Please take care and get better soon! Your friend, Jake C

Dave L – June 7, 2008
Sending love … send healing light

Dearest most gorgeous people … My thoughts are always with you, Michael … Lisa, Brian, Mary, and Jon. Of course precious babies Chino and Spresso! May you all be strong … in knowing we all are here … praying … and pulling for the courageous, tough young man. A testament to us all!! Daily! You all are so loved … and in the best hands! Sincerely and always, Dave

Jennifer K – June 7, 2008
Thinking of you!!

Dear Lisa, Michael, and family—
Hey, Lisa, this is your old pal from LeRoy Wade's fifth-grade class, not to mention Joan McGrew's third-grade class and Mrs. Imus's sixth-grade class (I think her first name was "Mrs."!). I just wanted you to know that I am sending good thoughts and prayers at least five times a day, maybe more! Your courage is an inspiration to all who know you. Keep up the fight, and I'll be in touch. You're truly amazing and strong! Love Jennifer

Mary L – June 7, 2008

Dear Michael and Lisa,
My heart is really hurting for both of you. Setbacks are hard to understand when you think you are getting some momentum. The good news is it was found right away. I'm believing it's early, not stage 4.

Lonnie L – June 7, 2008
Thinking of You

Dearest Michael and family,
God's power still prevails, and I will be beating down the door asking for that power to pour over you and the doctors. May you have a calm, peace, and clarity of mind that only God can bring. We love you very very very very much!! May our love help to bring you strength through these next few days.

Love,
Neil and Lonnie

Nancy Z – June 8, 2008
Heart of Courage

Michael,
We are so proud of you and the fight you are fighting. Your heart is full of courage and faith. We are praying for you all the time and you are never out of my thoughts. Lisa, keep up the faith and fight, you are the most awesome mom, and I love you very much. Let me know if there is any little thing I can do for you.

Love,
Nancy

Jen G – June 9, 2008
Thinking about you

Hi Michael,
This is crazy news, but we know that you will handle it as amazingly well as everything else that has come your way. You are so brave and tough!! We are thinking about you.

Lots of love, Doug and Jen

Nancy Z – June 11, 2008
You've Got IT!

Michael, you've got it—the strength and faith to fight on. Hope you know you have your whole family to support you. We are thinking and praying for you. Hope today goes well. Love you, Nancy

Lonnie L – June 12, 2008
Thinking of you

Dearest Michael,
It has been so long since I have seen you, and I missed that contagious smile, so I had to look through the photos! I hope I can see you next week. Until then, you are close to my heart, and the prayers continue to flow for every need. To tell you that I'm proud of you doesn't even begin to describe the admiration that I have for you. You are amazing. Thanks for being you.

Love Always,
Lonnie

End of CarePages.

After Michael was discharged from the hospital the following day, I called our radiation oncologist whom I was counting on to say something—anything—positive and give us a bit of hope. I left a voice message and expected a speedy reply due to the seriousness of the matter and his usual prompt responses. However, it was over three hours later when I received his call. I repeated the information I had left on his voicemail to be sure we were on the same page. After a very slight hesitation, he commented with a tone of seriousness, saying he had received my message shortly after I left it, but could not bring himself to return my call for these three hours. He knew our conversation would be difficult for me to hear and for him to relay. In his profession, certainly he must deliver difficult news on a regular basis, yet it struck me how he still had a compassionate heart that had not grown cold. "After reviewing the scan," he said, "I could see the tumor had blown out Michael's bone and broken it." He said they were able to keep one guy in a similar situation alive for a few years. The phrase "kept him alive" reminded me of the life we were leading now, with nonstop appointments, treatments, pain, procedures, and hospital stays.

At about this time, a cancer patient acquaintance visiting Michael at our home mentioned to him that she had gone to a healing room and received prayer, which seemed to help. I overheard this part of the conversation and immediately tuned into the discussion, recalling the books on healing I had read in the past and especially those about John G. Lake who had founded healing rooms many years before. Happy to learn there was one located in our area, I asked our visitor a few questions and decided right then and there that we would go.

After making several calls, I located the director of the Northshore Healing Rooms and briefly chatted with her about times, location, and Michael's worsening condition. She was very encouraging, and I felt hope rising up, which was a welcome contrast to what I had been wrestling with most recently. Michael was willing but didn't want to go since he was feeling weak, tired, and sick. The facility that housed the healing rooms was a chiropractic office by day and healing rooms by night several evenings a week and a few hours on Saturdays. Our first experience was interesting, and once again we seemed to be alarming people with our presence. Michael was feeling poorly, and it showed. He had a broken hip and could barely walk, but did so with a crooked, awkward gait which was far beyond a limp. He was thin, pale, wincing in pain, looked extremely fatigued, and as soon as he found a seat, he slumped down and dropped his head into his hands. The protocol was to sign in upon arrival. There was a waiting room where a receptionist sat at a desk. She was a smiling pleasant lady who greeted those coming through the front door and answered any questions. Soon each name would be called in the order it was received. There were three rooms in the back and two or three people in each who were ready to pray. When Michael's name was called, I was invited to go in with him, but I declined. I wanted to give him some privacy.

While I was seated in the waiting room, a young lady, also there for prayer, came across the room to sit with me and chat after Michael had gone to his prayer room. She said she'd had cancer eight years ago and had been coming to the prayer sessions ever since. She looked as healthy as anyone could possibly be, and I enjoyed her inspiring words as she told her story. There was beautiful instrumental music streaming throughout the room, and I felt myself relax as peace and comfort splashed over me. I was thankful for this oasis in the midst of our dry and bleak lives, for the young lady speaking her words of hope, and for the music, which seemed to escort God himself into this very room. Noticing the CD was for sale, I made the purchase and would have paid double the price for the comfort it brought. The CD became a daily piece of my life as I listened during my quiet time. I would turn it on and let the music bring the restoring power and presence of God into the room as He transformed the very atmosphere around me.

When prayers for Michael were concluded, he emerged from the room exhilarated and thanking those walking out with him, commenting on how he had felt God's presence in the room. It was a positive experience, and even though Michael was not healed physically, I do believe his emotional wounds were on the mend. The next Saturday, he still was not better, but worse, so when the prayer room opened again, we were there ready and waiting. He received prayer again with the same results. One of the men praying for Michael was Glen. He became a lifeline, calling Michael every day to pray with him over the phone. Glen became someone Michael relied on for sharing his feelings and receiving prayer, hope, and comfort through those calls.

When Monday rolled around, Michael was alarmingly worse, and when the healing rooms were opened once again, we were back. Michael was taken into the prayer room relatively quickly, and several of the healing room volunteers, including the lady at the front desk, were talking together and began discussing with me a revival going on in Florida. I had already heard about the revival and had watched it on the internet. It seemed many people were being healed. It started out as a one-weekend event but was continuing long beyond that time frame because of healings taking place and people traveling from all around the world to get there. When the prayers for Michael were finished, he returned to the waiting area and sat on a chair, exhausted and in pain. Then, as we were leaving, a lady, also a volunteer, looked at me and said, "If I were you, I would get on a plane and go." Her words resonated with something inside me, and I knew at that moment this was exactly what we would do—if at all possible.

CHAPTER 19

Desperate Measures— Flight East

BRIAN WAS IN AGREEMENT AFTER we briefly discussed a trip to the revival, so later that evening, I booked tickets for Michael and me. We would leave on Friday and come back Monday, as Michael had a doctor appointment Tuesday. Our airplane would take off from Seattle early in the morning, arrive in Denver where there was a short layover, and then we would begin the journey again, landing in Tampa in the early evening. Our car trip would be less than an hour to our final destination, but I reserved a hotel near the airport, not wanting Michael to have to make the additional car ride after the long day of airplane travel.

The Tuesday PET scan appointment right before our trip was a nightmare. Of course, Michael had had scans previously, so I knew approximately how long to expect him to remain in the scanning area. It was taking much longer than usual, and I was becoming concerned, so I asked the girl at the desk if she would check to see what was taking so long. She did and returned with the report that Michael was in so much pain he was having difficulty shifting and remaining in the various positions long enough to get the images. We were now charting new and enormously more difficult waters.

Unfortunately, just having gone through this with Mom, I was beginning to recognize stages and familiar landmarks. It is true that the types of cancer were different, but the path we were being dragged down was eerily similar to the one my mother had traveled, and I began to distinguish how far we had come and what was around that bend so close ahead. We had a small open window of opportunity before it would slam shut forever, and we had to get through the window and trust God for the rest.

On Wednesday, Michael had a chemo appointment, and once he was set up, I spoke with his doctor in the hallway, explaining to him about our trip to Florida. I asked if he could possibly give Michael some stronger pain medicine for the flight. I told him briefly that we were going to a Christian conference where Michael would get prayer. In response to my question, the doctor advised against such a long trip with Michael in his condition, but he would not say no. He continued to explain that he could not increase Michael's pain medicine dosage because he was already on the highest dose possible. Of course, I knew he could have more if he was under hospital or hospice care.

The next day, we received the results of the PET scan. It was worse than I had hoped, with not one cancerous tumor in his hip bone, but two, and they were quite large. The hip bone was definitely fractured, which we already knew. The doctor told us this cancer was now stage four-c rather than four-a because of the two extra tumors added to the equation. He told us they could do chemotherapy for about a year longer. That was good and bad, I was thinking. If things did not go quickly in the chemo's decimation of the tumors, it would be ending an important avenue of help when the year was up. On the other hand, Michael's condition seemed so bad already, enduring a year could be too difficult. Neither scenario felt hopeful.

That evening I called Rodica, who had previously been informed about the hip tumors, to let her know we were scheduled to go to Florida. I wanted to make sure she passed the message on to Lenuta, who now was staying with Cornell and Rodica. Lenuta was one who prayed, and I was glad to have her on board. Rodica was overwhelmingly in favor of the trip and told me a story of someone she had heard of who had been healed. This was encouraging, and I was confident she and Lenuta would continue to pray throughout the weekend, specifically about trip details, logistics, and Michael's healing. Not one of our relatives or friends advised us against going; rather, they reassured us that we should do what we felt we needed to do. We were very grateful for every word of encouragement, well wish, and prayer.

Michael was feeling terrible and still not eating, and we were back to getting all sustenance, including water, through his feeding tube. I was thankful the feeding tube had not been removed after the treatment of his throat. I felt he could make the trip, although it wouldn't be easy. Since he had not been working lately of course, he had no money except for small amounts of spending money we were providing him. Brian had the idea of offering him some bigger money—say $500—to buy something fun when he returned home. Even though Michael was willing to take the trip, this may just be the ticket to give him more incentive during the difficult times, which no doubt there would be, and to help keep his mind occupied having the entire trip to ponder and decide what to purchase upon returning. This was a brilliant idea and seemed to be working like a charm. Sure enough, Michael responded very favorably to the offer and was already coming up with good ideas for his purchases.

By Thursday evening I had our bags packed. We were taking only carry-ons as we had no time to bother with extra luggage. On the morning of June 13, 2008, I was up early preparing to go. Michael's feeding tube had been feeding him through the night, so I thought he should be fine. It was tough getting him out of bed and into the car as he was in pain and tired. Brian was driving us to the airport. We no sooner started the trek when Michael began protesting the speed, saying it was uncomfortable and painful when the car was traveling too fast. He asked his dad to please avoid accelerating or stopping quickly, but rather adjusting speed more gradually and slowly. Brian drove at a steady speed, giving himself plenty of room to come to gentle stops. It was an unnerving drive to the airport, but we arrived at last. Brian dropped us off at the entrance, and with promises to call him soon and final goodbyes, we were off.

Stepping inside the airport, I told Michael to have a seat while I located an agent and a wheelchair; however, Michael tried to follow, probably feeling he could manage, but he couldn't. I found an agent who came back with a wheelchair. Between Michael and I we explained how it worked. "Push slowly and steadily at all times. Do *not*," we explained emphatically, "go over any bumps. If there is an unavoidable bump it must happen very slowly and carefully with no sudden moves or jarring whatsoever." Our agent seemed agreeable but a bit alarmed with his new assignment. I slung my purse over my shoulder, grabbed the handles of the two carry-ons, and off we went at what felt like a turtle's pace. We had allowed plenty of time, so I had no worries about missing our flight. I couldn't help but notice the expressions of shock we received from those passing by, and I believe I also detected some disapproval.

We slowly arrived at our gate with time to spare. Michael passed the half hour or so trying to maneuver his wheelchair around a bit and headed down the corridor toward the restroom. I was nervous having him out of sight because of the condition he was in, and worried that the airplane doorway would open and wheelchair passengers would be called to board first. I tried to relax but found myself staring down the corridor watching for his return. It was a good thing, I kept reminding myself, that he was maintaining as much independence as possible and that he had the will to keep trying. I finally spotted Michael in the crowd making his way back. He had barely returned when the gate agent announced boarding was imminent.

We were among the first passengers on the plane and found our seats, which were quite far back because I had bought the tickets only earlier that week. Michael took the aisle seat so he could stretch out, encroaching slightly on the aisle. Hopefully his seating would also make for an easier departure when we landed in Denver where we were to catch our connecting flight to Tampa. This already seemed like a long day, and we hadn't even left Seattle. Finally, the plane took off, and there was no turning back. Michael was squirming in his seat, obviously uncomfortable, rubbing his hip. He wouldn't eat any kind of snack at all. He didn't want juice or water either. Although he had been fed and hydrated through his feeding tube during the night, I still didn't like it. Passengers were continually glancing our direction with the same expressions I described earlier. We weren't your usual everyday passengers, and the stares kept reminding us.

Michael tried to nap while I took the time to talk to God. I was glad for this time I could spend with Him because there was a lot to discuss, and I felt more peaceful and hopeful during and after talking to God. I was comfortable with my dialogues with Him because of His invitation in the Bible, to come and "reason together" (Isaiah 1:18) and to "Put Me in remembrance" (Isaiah 43:26). And so I began, "Lord, remember when I recently gave money for the building of a hospital wing? I know it wasn't much, but remember how you took the tiny lunch of the little boy and fed the five thousand? It's not the amount that is important; you proved that with the little lad's lunch. (John 6:10). Even a small amount makes a big difference as you bless it. I did it because I knew you needed people on earth to be your hands, and so I did it for you, for your children. And now, here I am, and my child is in need, and just as you needed me to help your children and I did, I need you to help mine. Lord, do you remember how the Egyptians were chasing the children of Israel and they were backed up to the Red Sea? Do you remember how fierce and frightening the enemy was that was coming to slaughter them? And how there was no way out for them, nowhere to go, and then you opened up the Red Sea and not only made a way for them to escape, but when they were safely through, you let the sea go back and the enemies who were pursuing them were drowned, never to chase them again? (Exodus 14:21–30). We are now backed up to our own Red Sea with nowhere to go, and the enemy pursues us relentlessly. Lord, make a way for us where now there is no way, and do away with our enemies so they can no longer come after us. Also, on another subject, you brought to us the topic of healing in the Bible. I am not making this up about healing. I probably wouldn't have thought of it, but I do now, because you brought it up first. Many times, in the Bible, you tell us you are the healer, and you will heal our diseases. This is why I'm praying for healing and why we are going for healing because you brought the subject to us (Psalm 103:1–5)."

This dialogue might sound presumptuous and unconventional, but the Bible says we are friends of God (John 15:15b) and can talk to Him, put Him in remembrance, and even reason with Him. There were other prayers on other days and lots of friends, family members, doctors, nurses, and acquaintances were praying as well, so my prayers were added to many other prayers.

At one point about midway during the flight, Michael got up and awkwardly made his way up the aisle to the bathroom and then back again. His appearance startled even me as he was walking back down the aisle. Perhaps it was the sunken eyes and the odd gray coloring that was the most concerning, even more so than the strangely thin and limping stature or the pinched look of pain in his expression or the helpless look in his eyes. This trip was harder on him than I had imagined. "God, he must receive healing," I shot out a quick prayer. "We can't take no for an answer." The reality was slamming into me that, without it, the trip home would likely be impossible. I had no idea I was not the only one having similar thoughts. One of my sisters later told me that, when she and her husband heard about our impending Florida trip, they did not believe we would be bringing Michael back.

After an excruciating and miserable flight, we were allowed to deplane before the other passengers, as our agent and wheelchair, which had been ordered in Seattle, had arrived and were waiting. The agent's assignment was to get us across the airport and to our departing gate for the remaining portion of our journey to Tampa. Unfortunately, there was not much time until take-off, and the gate was on the other side of the airport. It was a long trek, which added stress to an already unpleasant situation, as the time crunch became even more worrisome. Michael kept instructing the agent to slow down because of the level of pain he was experiencing, and he continued in his warnings about abrupt stops and possible bumps. Michael and the agent slowly and laboriously trudged ahead with considerable effort while I hopped aboard an adjacent moving walkway. I waited for them at the end of the transport section, having no choice but to be patient while continually and nervously glancing at the time.

We arrived at our gate with some time to spare, but I was concerned about this next portion of our journey. Michael was already looking much worse than he had during the morning flight. To get on another flight seemed really difficult. I stepped away from Michael and called Brian. I hated to give a bad report as he would be powerless to help, being such a distance away, but I did anyway. "This is not going well," I reported. "It's much worse than I imagined." After delivering my announcement with no nice tales to soften the facts, I told him we were about to board and would call when we landed. We did make a decision though. We decided that, before Michael and I got on the plane, I would give Michael the opportunity to bail out. After all, he was the one enduring the unimaginable, not us. If this was too much for him, we could get a hotel in Denver, rest, regroup, and make a decision from there. However, I knew Michael, so maybe I wasn't as open-minded and benevolent as it might appear. I knew he would want to continue on. He wanted to go to sunny Florida from rainy Seattle and on from Denver. He wanted to be healed, and of course, he was already making plans for spending his $500 upon returning. Michael was thinking life and the future, so I really wasn't surprised when he opted to continue on. His reasoning was that he wouldn't feel any better lying in a hotel. So, with our agreement in place, Michael and I boarded the plane for Tampa and found our seats toward the rear of the plane.

As we were resuming our usual positions with Michael in the aisle seat and me in the middle, I noticed a gentleman already sitting near the window in our row. I know this is not polite, but I decided to ignore him while we jockeyed into place, giving him not even a smile or especially any eye contact. While I normally would enjoy chatting with a random stranger nearby, I could not afford the luxury when there were additional discussions I intended and needed to have with God. These were crucial moments, and I had plans to stay focused and pray the entire flight. "Chatting is not allowed. Don't even start," I instructed myself silently. I also added a stern, unfriendly expression, firmly fixing it on my face to repel anyone from speaking to me. I was doing an excellent job on all counts, tending to Michael while ignoring the stranger. The plane was preparing for take-off and began its slow move into position. I had a fleeting desire to look toward the window, just a tiny glance without even a slight turning of the head. As soon as the thought struck, I took a peek, moving only my eyeballs, which wasn't quite sufficient, so I had to rotate my head ever so slightly. It was then I was met with sparkling friendly eyes, a broad smile, and a pleasant face catching my eyes and looking directly at me. "Are you wearing contacts or are your eyes really that blue?" "Well, I only wear one contact for mono-vision purposes, so I can both read and see distances without glasses." Gary Manos was an enjoyable, chatty guy, and I soon found myself caught up in his story on such subjects as his life, work, hobbies, children, and God. It was a pleasant distraction as we exchanged experiences and viewpoints. As I was enjoying the conversation, I reflected on my previous plans to spend the entire flight praying. It was at that moment that I sensed God's loving presence, like arms around me and heard his words speaking soothingly to my heart. "You have prayed, and I have heard you." I felt His smile and his reassurance that all was well.

We ended up annoying Michael, however, because napping wasn't easy with constant chatter going on beside him. He went up toward the bathroom again, and soon the flight attendant offered him an empty seat toward the front of the plane. Michael picked up his backpack and worked his way to his new seat assignment where he could stretch out and have some peace and quiet. He could get out of the plane more easily from there as well, and get to the bathroom more quickly—and have a much-needed break from me and my fellow conversationalist. As I could see Michael up those many rows, I felt an unexpected twinge of excitement and anticipation as I recalled that the healing room people had mentioned that some people were even healed on the way to the revival. The gentleman beside me and I were back full swing into chat mode, and he was talking about how he had blended his hobby of creating metal art into a business and now was enjoying his work while traveling and selling at various shows as well as on the internet.

CHAPTER 20

A Powerful Prayer

I WAS TOTALLY UNAWARE THAT, at that very moment, a change was taking shape, and unknown participants were beginning their entrance onto the stage of our lives. We were a little beyond halfway between Denver and Tampa as the drama was about to unfold and change our storyline forever. Gary and I were still chatting away in our seats when my eye caught someone toward the front of the plane. He was a tall man, maybe in his late fifties, standing in the aisle near Michael's seat. A woman was also standing nearby out of the aisle in front of the vacant seat directly behind Michael. This couple's attention was deeply fixed on Michael, and I could see the man was speaking to him. My mind was trying to warn me something must be wrong—an emergency of sorts—but my heart was strangely peaceful with no trace of fear or alarm. "The miracle we are coming for has begun" was my unexpected crazy thought as I sprang out of my seat and rushed toward the front. As I approached, I could see that the man had his hand on Michael's shoulder, and so did the woman standing behind Michael, and they were praying. It was a prayer of intense compassion, and the man's heart seemed to be breaking over the condition of the young person before him. I joined the circle and instinctively bowed my head. The prayer was filled with passion and boldness mixed with love, empathy, and authority. It was also combined with an indignation toward the cancer attempting to steal my son's life. As my head went down, I was stunned when I saw the man's tears fall past me and onto the floor as he continued. I don't remember the exact words, but I do remember the man not only prayed for healing but also was commanding the pain and cancer to go in the name of Jesus. As he prayed for Michael, he mentioned the blood of Jesus, which was referring to the blood that Jesus shed when he was crucified. The blood that He shed paid for our freedom and forgiveness from sin, brings us His power and gives us access to the promises of God. (1 Peter 1:18-19, Isaiah 53:5).

Finally, he paused and bent down to eye level with Michael. I bent down as well, eye level with both. First the man asked who I was. Then he asked Michael if he felt any better, and Michael answered, "Yes." The man asked him how much better, to which Michael replied that he felt about forty percent better. I was elated at the progress and turned to the man and said, "Keep praying." I wanted, of course, for him to continue until the answer was a hundred percent better! Just then, a young male flight attendant approached and asked if everything was okay. It was true, we had been causing a scene—not because the prayer or our conversation were overly loud, but because the close quarters made those nearby privy to even our quietest exchanges. As much as we were attempting to stay out of the way, we were guilty of blocking the aisle I supposed. I answered the flight attendant's inquiry by explaining that the man was praying for my son. I will never forget his gentle, kind response as he took a small respectful step back so as not to interrupt. He just said "Okay" with a nod of his head and asked if he could do anything for us. I responded by thanking him and could not think of anything we needed that he could supply at the moment. It was then that my eyes turned to the girl in Michael's row by the window and the passengers in the seat behind Michael as well as other passengers. I saw people crying and others dabbing their eyes or blinking back tears. I was touched by the compassionate, tender hearts and tolerance of the people surrounding us. I felt an earnestness to get the job done, however, so I swung my attention back to the matter before us and asked the man again to keep praying. But Michael put a stop to it. Later I found out that Michael thought I had persuaded this couple to come to his seat to pray for him. Furthermore, he observed, I was insisting the man keep praying, so I must be behind all this commotion. Attempting to set everyone free from the plot of his mother, he said he was tired and wanted to take a nap, and so he disbanded our little gathering.

I returned to my seat. I was filling Gary in when I felt a tap on my shoulder. I turned to see the man who prayed for Michael. He asked if I would come and join them in seats several rows back. I hopped up, cutting short my explanation to Gary, and followed him back. He offered me a middle seat, which I took, and he sat down on the aisle seat. I noticed the woman who had also been up praying was sitting across the aisle. We made introductions, and I learned the woman was Cathy Sampson who was married to Jeff Sampson, the man who had prayed. The other man next to me, near the window and also travelling with them, was Bruce Taylor. They were pastors and were on their way to the same revival we were planning to attend. They were going in order to learn what they could. As they spoke to me telling stories of healings and answered prayer they had experienced, I felt great hope rise as I pondered their words.

It seemed a little piece of heaven had unexpectedly dropped in on my parched, desolate existence. One thing Jeff said was that this illness was not anyone's fault. How interesting he should say that because many times I had wondered how this could possibly have happened. How could I, as his mother, have prevented this? I realized this was a question not even the doctors could answer, but my mind kept demanding to know, and so in many quiet moments, I found myself searching for elusive clues. I couldn't think of any environmental hazards he had encountered. There were always published articles about a high intake of vegetables preventing cancer. Could it be I hadn't given him enough vegetables? If my kids didn't like certain foods—usually the vegetables—I would make them eat two bites. My thinking was this would help them acquire a taste for the particular food, and they would be getting a bit of it, which was better than nothing. They ate lots of fruit though. I gave them daily vitamins and not too many sweets but wasn't as strict about the desserts with the younger kids as I had been with Jon. Maybe I should have been stricter. These were the thoughts that would come to haunt me from time to time, so I found Jeff's comment fascinating. Could this be God sending this message through Jeff?

He also made a random comment that Michael would sleep well that night. Why would he say this? Michael had not been sleeping well, and even if Jeff knew that, why would he choose that topic out of the many he could address? Jeff couldn't possibly know Michael usually woke up every two to three hours to take more pain medicine and could not get a lengthy, uninterrupted stretch of sleep. These remarks from Jeff were striking because he was addressing concerns that I had not disclosed to him, yet had been bothering me. It was as though God was speaking directly through him to me. *How tender and personally God deals with us*, I thought, and at that moment, God's presence felt so near and so sweet. Still in our seats, Jeff and Bruce prayed again for Michael, and I felt increasingly more refreshed and really didn't want to get off the plane at all.

Even so, the plane was nearing Tampa and soon started its descent. We had a smooth landing and rolled down the runway to our gate. The flight attendant invited me to proceed to the front before the other passengers left their seats so I could exit with Michael. I approached my former seat next to Gary, and he helped me with my bag. Then, with a serious expression, he handed me something and asked me to give it to my son. It was an attractive man's necklace—a cross made out of horseshoe nails suspended from a thick leather string. It appeared to be quite nicely made. I thanked him very much, wished him a good trip, and set off up the aisle toward Michael.

CHAPTER 21

Astonishing Change

WHEN I ARRIVED AT MICHAEL'S seat, I could see that the agent had brought the wheelchair onto the plane and positioned it near the beginning of the aisle. Michael made his way over and sat down. Before either Michael or I could rattle off the list of instructions, the agent made a sudden move, pulling the wheelchair backwards and over a large bump. It appeared to be two bumps together actually, where the plane and ramp joined together. Previously, Michael would have reacted in pain and doled out firm instructions on being careful when approaching and going over bumps. So, imagine my surprise when Michael was jarred over the two bumps together and said nothing. It was as if he hadn't noticed, but that was impossible. It was a larger bump by far than any of the others that had caused him to writhe in agony even when they were slowly and carefully breached. I made a decision at that moment to be an observer rather than a verbal participant in Michael's journey through the airport en route to the car rental area. The wheelchair assistant next took off like a race horse out of the gate, and Michael didn't seem to notice or care. First, he was jerked over a very large bump and then went sailing rapidly through the ramp enclosure from the plane to the airport. I can't imagine what my expression must have been as I was walking quite quickly, trying to keep pace while pulling the luggage and attempting to process what was unfolding before me.

It wasn't long before we were at the car rental area and the attendant left us to manage alone. I stood in a short line, received our paperwork, and then we were led a short distance to our waiting car. Michael got into the passenger side with no problem detectable to me and then helped me to program our hotel address into the GPS. I glanced at Michael as I was driving down the road, and he seemed better. He was helpful and interested in the surrounding areas we were traveling through. I asked him how he was feeling, and he said, "Fine." He never asked me to decrease the speed or break slowly when stopping. I left it at that and decided to watch and see what would play out rather than question him further, essentially assigning myself the dual positions of detective and eyewitness to this most intriguing turn of events.

Our hotel was nearby, so the long travel day was about to come to a welcomed end. We had no mishaps along the way. We settled into our hotel and found it to be pleasant, spacious enough, clean, and bright. Michael laid down on the bed, and I pulled out my MapQuest directions to Walgreen's, which I had printed out while still at home, and set out to get some Ensure for his feeding tube as he had not eaten all day. Upon returning, I immediately began preparing the feeding tube, feeling anxious about Michael's lack of food and water intake throughout the day. As I was about to pour the liquid into the bag, Michael stopped me. "Mom," he said, "I don't feel like doing the feeding tube tonight. Can I go down to the restaurant and see what they have?" This was yet another extraordinary development. I was trying to keep my excitement at bay, wanting to be an impartial observer and not an emotional parent, jumping to conclusions. I had made an additional purchase while at Walgreen's—a metal cane to assist with his limp. After I gave Michael the okay to check out the restaurant, he grabbed my credit card and his new cane, walked out the door, and disappeared down the hallway.

I called Brian while Michael was out of earshot. I had apparently saved all my emotion for him, as basically what he heard coming from my end was an exuberant, high pitched voice saying, "He's healed!

He's healed! I'm pretty sure he's healed!" I relayed the details of the happenings on the plane, the people we had met, and the changes in Michael. Brian was happy, relieved, and hopeful with uncertainty mixed in—much the same emotions I was feeling. Once off the phone, I tried to maintain my composure and return to the role of impartial observer once again. Time would tell for sure. I relaxed in the room, opened the curtains further, and let the sun stream in. After a bit, I heard a knock at the door. Knowing it would be Michael, I hopped up quickly to open the door, and there was my next big surprise. Michael was balancing his cane and two rather large Styrofoam dinner containers. He put the dinners on the table nearby, set his cane aside, and announced he had bought two barbequed rib dinners, one for himself and one for me. Michael picked up his dinner, propped himself up on his bed, leaned against the pillows, and opened the lid. Inside was a full meal including ribs, corn on the cob, fries, coleslaw, and a biscuit. I sat down on my bed and opened an identical meal for myself, but I couldn't stop gazing at the sight beside me. I will never forget how Michael took bite after bite as he devoured the entire dinner. I have no recollection of eating mine, although I did, but I do vividly remember watching Michael having his first normal meal in a very long time. What I didn't know at that moment was that Michael would never again use his feeding tube, and soon it would be removed for good.

When he was finished with his dinner, Michael went to the lobby. He was gone for a while, watching sports on the big-screen television. Upon returning to our room, he appeared energized, not exhausted after the long travel day. He seemed to be enjoying the new surroundings. He switched on the television and watched a few evening shows, changing channels between two or three he was interested in. I had my books to read, so I was content with whichever program was on and was basking in the joy that Michael was feeling better. I was having trouble concentrating on my reading, as I was reliving the day again and again—the dreadful morning commute, the torturous wheelchair ride through the Seattle airport, the stares, the miserable flights. That is, until the last leg when halfway through, suddenly everything changed.

I knew that a gigantic indicator for where we were on our newly spun-around journey would be how Michael slept during this night. Jeff had said Michael would sleep well, and I knew it would be significant if this were truly the case. Michael watched television until around eleven when he put the remote aside and we turned off the lights. I fell asleep easily but knew I would hear Michael if he got up. I had set my alarm, and when it buzzed in the morning and Michael was still asleep, I quietly got ready for my day, had a little quiet time with God, and prepared the maps and hotel paperwork. By this time, it was 11:30 a.m., and he was still asleep! We had to check out of the hotel by noon, so I woke Michael. I didn't think he had been awake during the night but wanted confirmation, so I asked him. Michael looked surprised as he thought about it and reported that he had not been awake or gotten up at all—and he had needed no pain medicine!

We checked out of the hotel, and Michael wanted to *walk* to a nearby restaurant that looked promising for a good breakfast. The day was bright and sunny with a brilliant blue sky. Colorful flowers bloomed in every direction I looked. I heard birds singing, and once again it felt as if the whole world was celebrating new life with us. I let Michael lead the way for a bit and watched him walk with barely a limp. When we got to the front of the restaurant, I asked him to turn around so I could take a picture. He turned toward me, smiled broadly, wearing his cross necklace from Gary. His eyes were gazing upward, and I snapped the picture. He looked relaxed and happy, no longer grimacing with pain in his expression and eyes. As I noticed customers coming and going from this busy little restaurant, I took note with amazement how Michael received barely a glance if any at all. Gone were the stares and the horrified expressions. Was that only yesterday? How could less than twenty-four hours change everything so drastically? How did one plane ride transport us from a life that felt like hell to a life that was like heaven? I could not keep my joy and relief in check. I continued, unapologetically, basking in it all and reliving it over and over in my mind.

We were seated quickly as this bright, clean restaurant was also efficient and roomy. We settled into our comfortable booth, and

Michael began looking over his menu. This time I was the one who kept staring at him. He ordered a large breakfast with eggs, sausage, pancakes, and juice. Then he began making calls on his cell phone. He was calling friends. We were so normal, so ordinary, and my emotions were soaring with gratefulness. Michael had a couple of brief conversations with friends lining up get-togethers upon our return. Soon our breakfasts arrived at our table. I remember nothing of mine except chewing and staring wide eyed as I watched Michael devour, with ease, his entire breakfast. Then to top it off, as we were finishing up, Michael remarked that he planned on buying some running shoes with part of his $500 when we returned home.

The revival was that evening, and I knew there were many people about to converge on the grounds hours early to hold their places in line. My plan was to rest up in the hotel and then arrive about three hours early. The grounds were large with people bustling everywhere. I found the entrance, saw the line, and followed it to the back so I could place myself in it. Michael would be joining me a little later. I always had at least one book in my purse, so I was looking forward to sitting on the ground with the rest of those in line and spending the time reading, but that was not to be. I was surrounded by ladies, and as soon as I sat down they began asking each other what had brought them to that place. As each shared her story, our newly formed group would pray for her need. The lady in front of me, named Shasha, had two young children with her and was very warm and supportive of each person. She stood out to me because of her caring manner. Also I thought she resembled our daughter, Mary. When it was my turn to share, the ladies rallied around me with expressions of concern, praying with an earnestness for Michael, his complete healing once and for all, and grace for our entire family. This was barely completed when Shasha spoke up and asked if Michael had a sister, to which I reported that he did. She said she felt God speaking to her, as we were praying, telling her that his sister was having a very hard time with all of this, even though she may not be showing it. I found this insight to be very helpful as she was correct in that Mary was not expressing her feelings about Michael's troubles much at all, and so I made a note to myself to attempt to draw her out more when we got home. After we waited for a long time on the grass, the door was opened for attendees to enter the air-conditioned tent and find a seat. The crowd poured in, and Shasha, her kids, and I sat down together. I saved a place for Michael and soon he joined us.

The lively service began with a few speakers. There was prayer and lots of singing. At one point the leader in front was preaching and pointed our direction and said that someone's left hip bone was being healed over there. I can be a skeptic with the best of them, but this seemed to be more than a coincidence. I hoped so anyway. The meeting was interesting as people lined up to get prayer from those on the stage, and there were ministry team members milling about praying for those who approached them for prayer. Michael got up from his seat and went over to a young man and woman prayer duo. I could see from a distance that he was sharing his request with them. They prayed a lengthy prayer for him, and the man gave him a big hug. I felt there was more than just physical healing taking place, but emotional healing as well. Shasha wanted more prayer for Michael, and even though she had come for her own reasons, she was, from the beginning, watching over us as well. She disappeared and returned with a small prayer team for Michael, and he received additional individualized prayer. Later we found out that Jeff and Cathy's daughter-in-law, Joy, was on one of the prayer teams so we had yet another Sampson praying for Michael!

When we arrived at the hotel after our exhilarating evening, it was nice to settle in and contemplate the interesting and rewarding day we had experienced. We woke late the next morning but had time to pack. I went down to the lobby for breakfast, but Michael opted to sleep longer; he would eat later. I was in line filling my plate with eggs, bacon, and a waffle when a man next to me in line, who was with his wife and two small children, asked what I was in town for. I replied that my son and I were there for the revival. He told me that he was a cameraman for the event. He asked where we were from, and we began a brief conversation. I explained where we had come from, why we had come, and since he seemed interested and the food line was slow, I gave him a quick synopsis on Michael and the encounter on the plane. He sprang to life with this new information and wanted to come to our room with his wife and the small grandchildren he was traveling with to pray for Michael. We sat down at our respective tables, and as I was finishing, I noticed him calling on his phone for others he knew to join the newly forming prayer team. But many of his colleagues were already gone, and it was left to him and his lovely wife to do the job solo.

When we entered our room, Michael was sprawled on his bed still half asleep. I introduced him to our guests, Jeffrey and Rachel, while Jeffrey was busy signing onto his laptop and inserting a music CD into the port. Beautiful music began filling the air in our little hotel room, ushering in the atmosphere of peace and rest, pushing away uncertainty and stress, which were always threatening to linger, right out the window. Our new friends began by anointing Michael with oil and praying with a heartfelt fervency I was in awe of, and then they turned their attention to me. I was to be the next beneficiary of their focus. I truly appreciated their warmth and continued enthusiasm in prayers for me. When the prayers were over, their little granddaughter, who was about five years old, handed a picture she had drawn to her grandmother and said it was for Michael. Rachel gazed at the sweet picture before her and noticed there was some printing on the picture—very neat hand printing in pencil by an adult, and her granddaughter had drawn the picture around it. It said "Happy Father's Day." When I looked at it, I assumed she had found a piece of paper that already had this written on it and she had drawn her picture anyway. Rachel kept her gaze on it. She seemed puzzled and said, "I wonder what this means." I couldn't see that it meant anything other than what I had already assumed, but she felt it had a prophetic meaning. She wondered aloud a few more times, and then a thought struck me. Maybe God was speaking again to Michael's future. Maybe there were plans in the making for his life on earth. This was not the end, but the beginning of a new and bright future with his own family and children. Michael took the picture and thanked the child for it. I was making a mental note to be sure it did not get left behind in our hotel room. It would be another powerful testimony to God's involvement, kindness, and power, and to this day I still treasure the drawing from our little prophetic artist visitor.

Jeffrey and Rachel left us, but not before Jeffrey whipped the CD out of his laptop computer and handed it to me. He said we could have the CD. He said he would have given us his computer too, but he needed it, which made me laugh. Of course, we would never have accepted his laptop, but the CD we received with thanks. Michael got up after our prayer time and was hungry, so while he was getting ready, I went to the lobby to get him some breakfast to bring back to the room. While I was there, I saw Jeffrey. I was beginning to dish up some food from the hotel breakfast buffet, but Jeffrey stopped me and ordered a huge specialty breakfast direct from the kitchen. I took the breakfast to Michael, and he ate it all.

We arrived home on a Monday, and Michael had a doctor's appointment on the following morning. It had been such a life-altering weekend that I hated that we would begin our routine with appointments at the hospital, but it had to be done. I dropped Michael off at the door while I parked the car, and I met him in the back of the cancer unit where he was getting his blood drawn. Next, we were given a room and told to wait for the doctor. Laurie was there, and soon a nurse walked in with his chart and the results from his morning blood draw. As the nurse entered the room, she glanced over at Michael and then stopped abruptly. She looked him over intently with an expression of surprise. I followed her gaze. There on the bed, in place of the pain-ridden young man with the grayish-colored face and exhausted, tormented eyes, was Michael reclining with his head propped up on a pillow, a smile on his face, a pink complexion, and alert eyes. He looked comfortable, pain free, peaceful, and friendly—like a new person. The nurse stood in front of him and asked, "What happened to you? You sure look good!" She checked his blood draw results and commented on how well his counts were looking.

Soon the doctor arrived, and the process repeated itself. He stopped in his tracks at his first glance in Michael's direction. He commented that most healthy people who traveled such a long distance and back in only a weekend would be exhausted. However, here was Michael looking as if he had spent the entire three days at a spa down the hall. Michael's scan had just taken place several weeks earlier, and so another could not be done until August, which was still two months away. It was a quick appointment, and we were soon on our way home. As amazing as all this was, the week ahead held more surprises. I felt again as if heaven was invading earth—at least our little section of it. Michael spent his week back home doing yard work and landscaping for money around home, pedal boating, playing basketball, and doing a little bit of jet skiing. It took me a day or so to descend from my cloud enough to realize I needed to call Rodica and let her know what had happened so that she could pass on the good news to Lenuta. I was so excited to make the call, and when I relayed to Rodica the details of our trip, the unusual events, and best of all, the undeniable and dramatic change in Michael, she was overjoyed.

The following is the CarePages entry I wrote after returning home from our weekend in Florida.

Posted June 19, 2008—10:49pm

I am sorry it's been so long since I have updated, but things have been changing very fast day by day. The PET scan showed two tumors in Michael's hip bones. These were good size, and he was very uncomfortable, so he was back on heavy-duty pain medicine. Our options were not many, or even sure possibilities. He had a round of "a new cocktail of chemo" last Wednesday, and life was miserable. The pain medicine wasn't doing the job, and more radiation was coming up.

A friend of Michael's mentioned a local healing room where a person can go just to be prayed for—a place where she had gone and experienced positive results. I had heard of these before and so, of course, we went. Some Christians prayed healing prayers for Michael and talked with us about a healing revival going on in Florida. Having reached the end of our ropes, we packed up, boarded a plane, and off we went.

We had so many amazing experiences. I could go into a million details, but the main point is this: God does heal. He is alive, well, and powerful. Michael got a lot of prayer. He even had incredibly bold and compassionate encounters with prayer warriors before even getting to the revival. And so, Michael has come back a changed person. His pain went away, his limp went away, his appetite came back, and his face is no longer drawn, but relaxed and happy. We ended up having a wonderful time in Florida. Michael was back to his former self, cruising around the hotel, ordering food, talking to people, and watching a game on TV in the lobby at the hotel. He bought some jogging shoes as soon as he got home and is planning some work options. The change in Michael is undeniable, and we are enjoying seeing him enjoy life again. We are, of course, continuing on with the recommended medical routine, but we are looking forward to the day when the doctors tell us we no longer need to come back.

Thank you again, everyone. Your prayers have proved to be invaluable. I feel as though you all filled up "the prayer bucket" with your prayers until it overflowed onto Michael, and we are thankful.

End of CarePages.

In 2011 Michael was doing the last of his scheduled follow up PET scans. It was during the summer of that year when I had to take my dad in for radiation for skin cancer. Michael's radiation oncologist was now also my Dad's. We met with him across from a familiar table in an office. When discussing Dad's situation a couple of times the doctor injected the question, "How is Michael?" I answer briefly that he was doing well and steered the conversation back to my Dad. I wanted to be respectful of the doctor's time, knowing he was very busy. He is a sought after and award winning doctor and we were just one of many who needed his time. After my Dad's situation had been thoroughly discussed he turned his attention back to me on the subject of Michael. He wanted to know more, so I began the story and told it all. His shocking response was the same I already had heard, but the words once again jarred me to the core. "Once the cancer returned Michael had less than a one per cent chance of survival." And then he added, "Not even that." He then remarked that how Michael was doing was well outside what medicine could do.

When Michael told his primary oncologist about what happened, and thanked the doctor for his part, the doctor replied, "It's not important to me who is in the credits as long as the Michael movie keeps playing." We really appreciate everything they did to get us where we needed to be to receive our miracle.

CHAPTER 22

Reunion with Lenuta

OUR REUNION WITH LENUTA HAPPENED shortly before the cancer was discovered in Michael's hip. It was an emotional evening for all of us. Lenuta was nervous and cried, and so did Mary. It was wonderful seeing her for the first time in seventeen years. The reunion took place at Cornell and Rodica's home where we had been invited for dinner. It was springtime, and we also enjoyed other times together—morning coffee outdoors at a nearby coffee shop with Rodica and her sister, Elena, and lunch at our home. Then came the following weeks, which were blurred with the new tumors, the new diagnosis, and our sudden trip to Florida.

We had returned home from Florida on Monday, June 16, 2008. The following Sunday, June 22, was Mary's twenty-second birthday as well as the seventeenth anniversary of the day we flew into Seattle from Romania with our two new family members. Lenuta wanted to make Mary a birthday cake, so it seemed fitting to organize a party. We had so much to celebrate. Mary and Michael wanted to have friends over to meet Lenuta, and so did Brian, Jon, and I, so the guest list kept growing as we attempted to finalize our party plans. It was a happy week full of life and promise. Once again, we could have parties to celebrate events, friendships, and family.

The day of the party arrived, and it was all I imagined it to be. The house was soon filled with friends and family members, and what a joyous celebration it was. Lenuta brought her cake, and the smell of barbeque was in the air. She was introduced to guests. We had a lovely and lively time. The competition and performance jump rope team Mary had been on while in school had become quite well known, having competed nationally and internationally. Her team won first place spots and brought home large trophies for their hard work. Mary had also competed with an individual routine she created, which earned her an interview on ESPN when she was fifteen. We were well into the party when Mary and several of her jump rope team friends were asked to perform. So they decided to have an impromptu, short performance on the patio to show off a few of their skills. The house emptied as we all filed out the doors and gathered around the girls who were in place. Two held the double-Dutch ropes, one on each end, and two were poised to enter the ropes. The turners began rotating the ropes, increasing the speed and settling into a quick rhythm as the jumpers were preparing their entrance. It was at this moment a voice in the crowd boomed out, "I'm coming in!" Michael emerged from among the guests, rushed past everyone, and jumped into the turning ropes. He jumped and spun around in sync with the tempo of the swirling ropes, and my mind flashed back to slightly over a week before when we were struggling through the airport with a wheelchair and a broken hip. It was a startling moment, as I had no idea he could jump double-Dutch at all, even before cancer and a broken hip. I stood there speechless, barely comprehending what I was witnessing. This was all God's show, and a stunning one it was.

July came to a close, and the warm days of August were upon us, and then came the PET scan appointment. It was a much different experience than the June scan when Michael's actual scanning had lasted unusually long because of the discomfort and pain level. What a nightmare that day had been. On this day, when he zipped through relatively quickly, we were delighted. It would take several days, of course, to get the results back, and so we waited. The difference in Michael was obvious, yet to see it on paper and have proof was something we were excited for. It was a nerve-wracking wait, and I had to keep my attention on what had taken place, on how Michael was doing now. I had to focus on the promises in the Bible and not on the fear that was ever nearby, waiting to pounce and take us down.

One of the last of my CarePages entries tells the story.

Posted August 13, 2008—11:10 p.m.

Today has been one of those days that will go down in our family's history as unforgettable—one that will be relived over and over in our memories, I'm sure. Today was the day of the PET, CT, and MRI scan results. We had seen the transformation in Michael during our Florida trip; that transformation remained, and Michael grew stronger, but today it is on paper. Today it came from the doctor's mouth—complete remission! And from the written words on the PET scan report: "No PET CT evidence of active residual disease."

The PET scan is performed to detect the presence of cancer in the body by measuring metabolic activity, particularly in a tumor. The patient is first injected with a mixture of water, sugar, and radioactive material. Cancer cells will gobble up the sugar solution complete with radioactive material causing any suspect area to glow, consequently revealing metabolic activity that can indicate the presence of cancer. This metabolic activity is measured with units called SUV which stands for "standard uptake value." Any SUV measurement in the body having more than a three level is considered hyper metabolic. The PET scan is combined with a CT scan, which can help to further define what is going on in the body and what is causing an area to be hyper metabolic if that should be the case. Michael's doctor told us that the normal SUV range is one to three.

As the doctor read the report, he explained that Michael's SUV counts of the two tumors, previously had been 17.3 and 16.3 at the point of the PET scan done on June 10. In the PET scan taken last week (August 6) cells in the areas where the tumors had been, showed a 1.4 SUV, well within the normal range. What a change! We had a day of celebration, and it was Jon's birthday on top of it all.

The feeding tube was eliminated on July 21, and it was so easy I kept trying to make it harder. Michael's name was called for the outpatient procedure in the diagnostic imaging department at the hospital, and less than ten minutes later we were walking out feeding tubeless and quite surprised. If only everything were this easy! It went something like this: The doctor doing the procedure called Michael's name in the waiting room. We all three walked in. Michael laid down on the table and asked what it feels like to have it deflated (first step to removal is the deflation of a little balloon that holds the tube in) to which the reply was that he had already deflated it. The next question from Michael was "What does it feel like having it pulled out?" To which the doctor replied, "It's already out." So, being unable to accept that *anything* in life, let alone in a hospital, can be so easy, I asked if he should refrain from showering or swimming, to which the doctor replied that it probably would be a good idea to wait for a few days. Okay, so I made it a little harder, but still that wasn't too hard, so I asked if we should be changing the gauze soon, to which he replied that we could if we wanted to but probably wouldn't need to, and that the small abdominal opening would close by itself quite quickly, no stitches, no special treatment or special care, just remove the gauze in a day or two and that's it! A little bit of medical trivia is that, apparently, according to a nurse, stomach muscles are one of the fastest healing areas of the body. This is an interesting surprise fact that made our lives a little easier.

Thank you for your prayers, which helped again to bring us the good news we have today.

End of CarePages.

CHAPTER 23

Conclusion

MICHAEL NO LONGER NEEDED MEDICATION for pain, but getting off pain medicine is not so easy. Kicking a drug dependency can be extraordinarily difficult. Michael was tapering off the drugs, mostly under his doctor's supervision, but this process proved to be slow and painstaking and an up-and-down process as his dosage had been so high. We were all in a battle together fighting some really powerful forces, and at long last he was off the drugs. During this time, Michael was also facing some other challenges I could not have imagined. He had been living in a different world than his peers, as they were still mostly carefree, had been completing college, dating, growing up, and maturing. They were enjoying life, as many young people do, with the optimistic outlook that told them they were fairly invincible and their lives would unfold almost perfectly. Michael, however, had come face to face with an enemy no one wants to see no matter what age they are, and that confrontation told a very different story. It took time for him to overcome the feeling of vulnerability. In the end, Michael prevailed with God's and the doctors' help and was completely free from addicting pain drugs. I can remember during these years that I knew God was with us during our trouble (Psalm 91:15), which helped because Michael's struggles during that time period were very difficult.

And so it was one day at a time, one verse at a time, one promise for that day, and these I would try to hang on to. How many times had I heard from doctors, nurses, pharmacists, and medical technicians "The statistics show ... this is where we go next ... and these are the side effects ..." I knew all these statistics were correct, *but* it says in the Bible to cast down every high and lofty thing that exalts itself against the knowledge of God (2 Corinthians 10:5). So, I was to cast down the statistics in my mind and focus on the knowledge of God, which was the fact that He does heal. I determined, to the best of my ability, to focus on these truths. Some people had commented that I was strong. I was not strong. But when I kept my eyes on Him and His promises, I would not fall into the pit of bitterness and misery that seemed to have no bottom, for this I was most afraid of. I could not allow myself to fall off that edge. If I did, I feared I would never be able to crawl out again. The safest place was to turn to God and not away during these difficult times.

So, it was a great delight to see Michael happy, enjoying friends and church life again. In December 2014, six and a half years after our trip to Florida, Michael was asked to give his testimony at a church. He had become known for his serving and also for his lively, joyful worship. Of the three services—the youth service on Saturday night and two services on Sunday morning—it was the Saturday evening young adult service, which usually had about 250 in attendance, where he would speak. His presentation was to be short, only a little over five minutes long, and it wasn't a big deal, but to me, it was monumental. It truly was, in my way of thinking, a milestone for all of us, and I was delighted that we were to be in the audience. I had told our story over and over throughout the years. But this was much different. I was proud of Michael and how he had turned to God and was now beginning to articulate his story. But it was much more than that. He had developed a deep passion for people, especially the hurting ones. He would offer support and prayer to those he met along the way who were sick, homeless, or defeated in any way. His suffering had produced a depth of feeling that enabled him to share the hurts of others.

Brian and I arrived for the service, and I was amazed at the number of people attending as well as the welcoming atmosphere at the entrance to the sanctuary where there was a table laden with plates holding heaps of cookies alongside urns of coffee, tea, and water. We moved into the seating area and found it to have a vibrancy and energetic feel. People milled around greeting one another while finding seats. Michael kept bringing different friends over to introduce us, which was a delight as we had heard many of these names previously and already felt a warmth toward them. Michael had prepared for this opportunity by outlining his main points and typing them into his phone so he could speed through the talk more efficiently while staying on point.

The worship team took their places on the stage and soon were singing and playing instruments while the crowd enthusiastically joined in. After worship, the youth pastor began to share, and then came testimonies. A lady who worked at the church told her story first, and the pastor spoke again. Finally, on cue, Michael walked onto the stage. He looked strong, healthy, and confident, and yet a little nervous. He began relaying the much-abbreviated version of a dramatic life, beginning in Romania, touching on a few of the many pieces that came together in an unlikely fashion to allow his exodus from the poverty left over from communism, and an abusive stepfather into a life of opportunity and freedom. The notes disappeared when his phone went dark on stage a few sentences in, and rather than fiddle around with it, he abandoned his phone notes and began speaking from his heart, which, to me, was better anyway. He went on to share the story of his struggle with addiction in high school, going to rchab, and then, one month after turning twenty, receiving his cancer diagnosis. He talked a bit about the difficult cancer treatments, the trip to Florida, the plane ride, and the prayer from Jeff and Cathy and others who prayed. Next, he shared his remarkable recovery, detailing how these experiences, along with witnessing the power and love of God, created in him a passion to know God more deeply. He did a great job, and at the conclusion, the crowd stood up and clapped and cheered enthusiastically as Michael walked off the stage.

It was Jesus they were giving the standing ovation to, and there was a celebratory mood in the room as the applause continued. Next the worship leader began to speak again. "You never know the reason someone dances," he said, "and so you might think, *Man that guy over there, he's a little crazy … but he's got some stuff to dance for in his life.*" The audience was still clapping as he continued, "So, Michael, we are going to dance. We are going to end this with a dance song." And so it began—a lively song with the people jumping up and down dancing, raising their clapping hands as they sang loudly, "Thank you, Jesus! Thank you, Jesus!" to the music of the guitars and other instruments on the stage. It was an awesome moment that finally came to a close as the song concluded and the youth pastor came forward to dismiss the people. As he came on stage, he said he had grown up in that church and had never seen anything like that celebration before.

A short time later, near Christmas, the senior pastor was giving a sermon on joy. It is the custom in that church to invite people to share short testimonies during the service, as Michael had done for the youth service. But this time Michael was asked to give his talk during the two Sunday morning services. One service would have approximately one thousand in attendance, and the other about 750. This time we invited family members to attend, and so we came with our own personal crowd to add to the event. We loved visiting and were touched by the overflowing pile of new backpacks loaded with supplies for the underprivileged, which were heaped on one side of the foyer. We were also touched by the cheery Christmas decorations, the coffee bars, and the smiling people. It was a welcoming, lively environment, and we were enjoying our visit. An inspiring sermon on joy was delivered, and midway through, Michael was introduced as an example of one who carries joy. He walked onto the stage and shared his story. To us, as his family, who journeyed this road alongside him, it was another huge and significant life milestone.

Michael did an outstanding job, and once again came the applause as the people hopped to their feet as before. It was clear that this jubilant response was directed toward Jesus for His power and great love. It was thrilling and emotional to see Jesus being honored and celebrated, for this was His story.

I couldn't help but reflect a bit on our long and messy journey. By messy I mean the imperfect way we traveled these paths that were sprawled out before us, each toting along our own particular flaws, traumas, and baggage. As we step out to do something difficult, beyond where we are comfortable, with tasks greater than our abilities in an effort to change our circumstances, our weaknesses become evident. Maybe this story began with Lenuta and her call out to God to save her children, or with Cornell, who risked his life for the start of a new one in a foreign land. Whatever the case, this story of challenge and hardship, with participants from around the globe, became a testimony of the involvement of God who hears our cries and sees our struggle. He is an expert at putting broken pieces together, no matter how scattered and scarred, in a much better arrangement than we could ever dream or imagine.

Primarily, what stands out and touches me the most is how ready He is to take the journey with us if we will turn toward Him and not away. He forgives failings, He comforts, encourages, changes outcomes, forms new paths, connects us to amazing people, heals the hurt, and gives strength. All our journeys are different. Getting on a plane to a healing revival obviously is not everyone's answer, but a relationship with Jesus always is.

Message from Cathy Sampson Whiteaker

Hi, Lisa...What an awesome God we have. Our story began in 2004 I think when we first attended Bethel Church in Redding and were inspired to start praying for the sick wherever we might meet them. So Jeff and I often prayed for people out in public. On that day on that airplane, of course, we were headed to Lakeland, Florida to get more equipping to pray for the sick. We were farther back in the airplane, but we both saw Michael as he went into the restroom and walked back to his seat. He was in OBVIOUS pain and distress and needed assistance as he went back to his seat. We asked the stewardess what was wrong and I think, she just mentioned cancer. So Jeff looks at me and I look at him and we say we need to go for it. Jeff always said, "Let's go for it. You know how to spell FAITH, R-I-S-K." Jeff said he would go up and ask Michael if we could pray for him and then he would call me up if it was a go. So of course, Michael said yes, and we just started to pray for him in his seat. It felt like the Presence of God came down and was very heavy around Michael and for a few seats around him. It was a pretty short and simple prayer, but obviously, the Lord healed Michael from that moment on. We didn't know he was being healed, but the power of the Lord was obvious to us. Then we went and sat down and you, Jeff, and Bruce started to chat about what was happening. The last we thought we would see of Michael was him being wheeled off the plane in a wheelchair. The next day at the meeting we saw Michael walking around and praising God with his arms raised. I told Jeff, "Look there is Michael. Amazing." Then Joy and her friend prayed for Michael too. It was a family affair. Of course the rest is history. Thank you Lord. What an honor to pray for Michael. You never know what God will do when you pray, and that moment on that plane it was done. If there is anything else you want to know, just ask. I am certain if Jeff were here, he would write three pages for you. He always remembered all the detail. Have a perfectly awesome Thanksgiving. Love you and your family.

Cathy Sampson Whiteaker
November 22, 2014

Message from Carol Thielke

I never prayed for Michael, as I was on the desk most of the time. I do remember that he would lie in the car until it was time to be prayed for because he was in so much pain. When he did come in, it was evident that he was in a lot of pain. I remember that Margie and I told you about the revival in Florida that was having a lot of healing testimonies because Michael seemed to be getting worse. I did not hear anything else until you brought him in after your return home. It was very obvious that he had been healed, and it was so thrilling to hear what happened to him on the way to Florida. When he joined our team as a volunteer, it was faith building to the people he prayed for as well as the team. His testimony is one of the most dramatic that I have personally been involved in.

Carol Thielke
North Shore Healing Rooms
August 25, 2016

OTHER PERSPECTIVES

Bruce W. Taylor, archbishop of the Province of St. John of the Cross, counselor at Veterans Readjustment Counseling Center (passenger on flight UA1612 from Denver to Tampa).

Michael looks a lot different from that young guy in agony aboard that plane on our way to Tampa! Cathy and I will never forget. Jeff is now in that great cloud of witnesses above, but I'll bet he still watches over Michael just as he watches me. He still has my back as always and Michael's too. None of us will ever forget!

Cathy Sampson Whiteaker, retired Speech Language Pathologist (passenger on flight UA1612 from Denver to Tampa).

I remember feeling like the Holy Spirit just fell heavily all around us. Several people sitting close by were weeping as the Holy Spirit's presence was so thick. Wonderful memories. Much love.

Gary Manos, owner of Steel Knight Designs (passenger on flight UA1612 from Denver to Tampa).

I feel truly blessed to have been a part of that day/ flight! I love that Michael continues to wear his cross necklace. I have a new one now, and anxiously await who the next recipient might be. You know, maybe you should write a book? It could give real hope to those who might be going through what you, Michael and your family went through. I think hope is one of the best things we could give to anyone. Hope leads to dreams...dreams lead to ideas...ideas lead to action...action leads to results! It's just a thought Lisa, but I think you'd have quite a story to tell. I think people love triumph in the face of adversity! I am blessed with getting to be a part of that amazing day and flight!

Jeffrey Levinson, GOD TV, Marketing/ Special Projects/ Strategic Partnership/ some producing.

This young man, Michael came with his mom to the Lakeland Revival in 2008 because he was battling stage four cancer that had gone into his bones and exploded his hip bone. Rachel and I were at the Marriott... we met his mom while having breakfast. She told us the story how they were watching the Revival and decided to take the long flight east. We said we will be down here, come and get us when he wakes.... we brought music and olive oil and prayed for him almost 2 hours. We were back downstairs and his mom came back down. We had the chef make a huge breakfast, he ate it all...... fast forward today his faith and that of his mom Lisa Bate's faith he was made whole.... Praise the Lord for he is healed!

Joy Sampson, from the Facebook live Happy Hour broadcast with Nathan and Joy Sampson.

My favorite God story is when Michael got healed of cancer. He was a stranger to us. I could even cry now how God orchestrated it to where our whole Sampson family could share in it. Michael was on a plane to Lakeland, Florida and while he's on the plane he met Nathan's parents and they prayed for him. Michael had metastasized cancer that went to his bones and he had a bone that exploded and was broken and he was in excruciating pain. Nathan's parents prayed for him on the plane and he immediately fell asleep. That night he ate a big dinner after being on a feeding tube and not eating. It amazes me, it makes me want to weep just thinking about it. He was healed on the plane and then he was out of the wheelchair, and walking with a cane. I didn't know the story at all. I was there with a group of girlfriends. We volunteered to be on the prayer team. My friends and I were prayer partners and here he comes walking up to us. I think he was still in the middle of being healed. I think it was a rapid progression, but when we saw him we thought oh this kid looks so sick. He was limping up to us on the cane. He looked gray and I thought, do I have the faith? When we prayed, he just started turning pink and his face looked like it was plumping up and you could see God all over him. A couple of hours later I saw him coming through the prayer tunnel and I said. "Michael, where is your cane?" and he said, "I don't need it," and he was literally walking without a limp through there. I didn't know then that Michael and Lisa previously had contact with Mom and Dad, and exchanged emails. I found out later from Mom, that Michael was out playing basketball, and his PET scan came back clear. Miracle. And guess what, it never came back and he is healthy today. It's been twelve years. He sat in our living room two years ago. And he ate dinner with us and I'll never forget this story. I will cling to it because God heals. And it was literally amazing. I love how both myself and my father and mother in-law got to meet this guy and God encouraged our lives and changed our lives through that.

Lonnie Lennebacker, bookkeeper, mom, and grandma.
So thankful for God's touch of healing upon Michael. The lives that have been and will be blessed and strengthened by his testimony are vast. It was such a blessing to be with Lisa, Michael and the family and witness the power of prayer.

Nancy Zombro, Lisa's sister and Michael's aunt.
I remember when Michael was diagnosed with cancer, it was such a shock as he was so young. Then as time and treatments went on and he grew worse with the cancer metastasizing in his hips, it did not look good. His parents did everything medically and spiritually they could think of. My sister Lisa is a strong woman of faith and her perseverance paid off. God responded and healed Michael on a plane trip to Florida. He came back home to be jumping rope in a week, totally healed. A true miracle from God. Love you Michael!

Laurie Davies, retired LPN, Lisa's sister and Michael's aunt.
What an amazing miracle and what a blessing! I had never witnessed a miracle so big before this. What a difference in Michael before and after that trip to Florida. Praise the Lord for his blessing of healing. We love our Michael!

Jane Krpan, Lisa's sister and Michael's aunt.

We were so happy when Mary & Michael joined our family from Romania, so to have Michael diagnosed with stage 4 cancer was devastating. I saw Michael at death's door with my own eyes, right before his trip to Florida. I couldn't imagine how Lisa would manage the trip with him on her own, but she was determined. When I saw him next, there was no doubt that a profound miracle had occurred! He was healed & on the road to a full recovery! Such an amazing story!

Paul Graves, close friend.

Michael's story is just about the most incredible miracle I've ever known. It spurs my spirit, strengthens my soul, fuels my faith to continue to "see" what I cannot see.

EPILOGUE

OVER TWELVE YEARS HAVE PASSED since the day on the airplane. Michael has remained completely cancer free. Scan after scan came back clean until at last we were done. He recently graduated from the University of Washington, is newly married to Taryn Bate, and is now ready to embark on a whole new chapter of life with career, family, and whatever God has in store for him. He is passionate about God and wants to be in ministry as well as in business. He is always busy with friends, church, family, and work.

During the time of Michael's treatment Jon was temporarily living at home because he was remodeling his house. It was great to have his help and support during that time. Brian and Jon are partners in our construction and maintenance business, and it has been a joy to work with Jon through the years. Jon is married to Kaitlyn Bate, and they have a young son named Beckham and a new baby daughter named Blakely.

Mary was also living at home during Michael's treatment and working through a temp agency at Microsoft while finishing her last class at the University of Washington. She has now been working at Microsoft for ten years and is married to Shannon Phillips. They also have a young son. He is named Levi and is one month older than Beckham. Mary and Shannon are now expecting their second child. We all live relatively close to each other and we are really enjoying these grandkids.

This whole experience led Brian to step back and reevaluate his life. The reality of Michael's illness and healing had a profound impact on him. He has had his own new encounter with Jesus and it has changed him dramatically. It made me think back to the prophetic word from the man I spoke with on the prayer line. We obviously had the life changing experience he predicted, so I decided to call back to tell them of our answered prayer. The woman who took my call that day was intrigued when I gave her the details and she looked back on the record of my call, which was there, with my name, the date, and the prayer request listed. However, the man who prayed that day never entered his name. That space on the form was left blank. She had no idea who he might have been.

Cornell and Rodica have three grown sons, own a thriving business, and are very involved with their church. They go back to visit Romania often and recently funded and completed the construction of a church building in Somesu Rece.

Jeff Sampson checked up on us regularly by phone after our meeting on the plane, until he went to heaven in 2011. Cathy and I have remained friends and are in contact through Facebook. She eventually met and married Bruce Whiteaker, and they both pray for Michael regularly. Michael has visited them in California.

Gary, the man sitting next to me in the airplane and who gave Michael the cross necklace, and I are occasionally in touch through email and Facebook. He is doing well in his metal art business, and his kids are now grown.

Jeffrey and Rachel Levinson will always be special friends to us, and we stay in contact through Facebook. I have loved watching their two grandchildren grow through the pictures they share. After our Florida trip, Michael and I took another trip back later that summer, and Jeffrey Levinson, being a cameraman for the revival event, saved us some great seats right up front and arranged extra prayer for Michael. He even got us a pass to eat in the back room with the crew.

Gheorghe passed away in Romania several years ago, and Lenuta still lives in Somesu Rece. She lives in the family home, and her grown kids live in Cluj-Napoca.

And as for me, I'm excited about following where the Lord is taking us next. I know He has a great plan, and I'm looking forward to the adventure!

Blessings,

Lisa Bate

lisadianebate@gmail.com

Saturday coffee with Mary, Lisa, and Lenuta.

Michael, ready for breakfast our first morning in Florida.

Lunch later that day.

Michael with the cross necklace given to us on the airplane.

Brian and Lisa.

Jon, Kaitlyn, Blakely and Beckham Bate.

Mary, Shannon and Levi Phillips.

Taryn and Michael Bate.

Lisa and Michael's boarding passes from
Denver to Tampa, June 13, 2008.

Taryn and Michael on their wedding day.
Photo credit: Thien Lai.

Printed in the United States
By Bookmasters